A Group Leader's Guide to

Brief Strategic
Problem-Solving Group Therapy:

Making Group Therapy Work in the
Managed Care Environment

A Group Leader's Guide to

Brief Strategic
Problem-Solving
Group Therapy

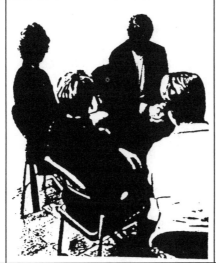

Making
Group
Therapy
Work
in the
Managed
Care
Environment

By Terence T. Gorski

Based on the CENAPS Model

Herald House/Independence Press
Independence, Missouri

Copyright 1995
Terence T. Gorski
18650 Dixie Highway
Homewood, IL 60430
Phone: 708/799-5000 (FAX: 708/799-5032)

Additional copies may be obtained from the publisher:
Herald House/Independence Press
3225 South Noland Road
P.O. Box 1770
Independence, MO 64055-0770
Phone: 1-800-767-8181 or 816/252-5010 (FAX: 816/252-3976)

Printed in the United States of America
ISBN 0-8309-0716-5

99 98 97 96   2 3 4 5   17-026062

Table of Contents

CHAPTER 1

Group Therapy in the New Era of Treatment

The chemical dependency and behavioral health field has changed. A powerful move toward cost containment has forced an administrative and clinical restructuring of group and individual therapy services. Clinicians who can adjust are finding exciting new opportunities providing brief strategic therapies. Those who can't or won't are finding their careers in jeopardy.

Two factors are responsible for these major changes: the widespread use of managed care organizations (MCOs)[1] to control the cost of behavioral health care; and the growing sophistication of the consumers of chemical dependency and behavioral health services. Both factors have forced group and individual therapy to change from a long-term, supportive, loosely structured process to a targeted, strategic, short-term, and outcome-oriented process.

Driving Forces in the New Era

1. Managed Care Organizations (MCOs)
2. Sophisticated and Demanding Consumers

Because most MCOs have the power to approve or deny payment for treatment, they have a powerful influence on the type of interventions used by treatment providers. Their definite preference is for therapies that provide quick assessments and no-nonsense treatment plans that can be administered in twelve to twenty sessions.

Consumers of treatment services are also getting more sophisticated and demanding. Because they are being forced to pay for a larger share of the treatment, many people are unwilling or unable to pay for months or years in long-term therapy. They want to get results quickly and efficiently, and they know that it is possible. Information on brief therapy is readily available in most bookstores and discussed in detail on many of the most popular talk shows.

When designing group therapy programs it is important to understand the basic requirements of both MCOs and the new generation of sophisticated and demanding consumers. Many of these requirements have significant impacts on the delivery of group therapy services. Once these requirements are understood, brief strategic problem-solving group therapy systems can be implemented that can meet these needs.

What Are the Needs of Managed Care Organizations?

Although each MCO operates according to its own unique set of criteria and practices, several general characteristics are emerging that accurately describe most progressive managed care companies. Most MCOs want treatment that is targeted, strategic, time efficient, and based on cognitive and behavioral therapy principles. **Targeted treatment** quickly identifies the core issue that will be the focus of the current treatment episode. **Strategic treatment** identifies a concrete goal for the current treatment episode and develops a specific series of interventions that are directly related to achieving that goal. **Time-efficient treatment**, often called brief therapy, uses directive therapy techniques, therapeutic assignments, involvement in low-cost psychoeducation programs, and self-help group attendance to accelerate the treatment process while lowering the cost. **Cognitive behavioral principles** identify and change the thoughts, feelings, behaviors, and relationship styles that drive the target problem.

12

```
┌─────────────────────────────────────────────────────────┐
│                                                           │
│         The Type of Therapy Required by MCOs              │
│           •  Targeted                                     │
│           •  Strategic                                    │
│           •  Brief and time efficient                     │
│           •  Based on cognitive and behavioral            │
│              therapy principles                           │
│                                                           │
└─────────────────────────────────────────────────────────┘
```

Most MCOs require quick up-front assessments that identify: (1) the *presenting problems* (Why did you seek treatment now?); (2) *related disorders* (physical, substance use, or mental disorders; or situational life problems) that are contributing to the presenting problems; (3) the *current level of dysfunction* caused by the presenting problem and related disorders; and (4) the *target treatment problem* that will be the central focus of the current episode of treatment; (5) a concrete *outcome goal* that describes what will be accomplished by the treatment process; (5) a specific series of *interventions* or action steps that will be used to accomplish that goal in a time-effective manner; and (6) documented *progress reports* of what is being done to help the patient complete the action steps of the treatment plan and how the patient is responding.

Although these requirements are reasonable and make sense, they are often difficult to meet, especially when the majority of treatment is being administered in group therapy sessions. This is because many group leaders have difficulty keeping their groups focused on the interventions described in the individual treatment plans of group members. As a result they often have difficulty getting reimbursed for group therapy services.

Group Therapy Services in the New Era

What is needed is a brief strategic problem-solving group therapy procedure that will allow group members to work on target problems by implementing a sequence of preplanned interventions. This strategic group therapy process must allow the therapist to plan and track the implementation of individual treatment plans across a series of group therapy sessions. This means each group member will be working on different individual treatment plans at the same time.

The good news is that this style of group therapy is well received, not only by MCOs but more importantly by the group members receiving the service. Group members learn to rapidly identify the goals they want to accomplish and stay on task until they have achieved them. They have a clear set of group skills they can learn that allow them to work more effectively and efficiently in their groups. As a result they are more satisfied with their progress than with many other forms of group treatment.

The Purpose of This Book

This book will show you how to run brief strategic problem-solving group therapy sessions. It focuses on practical techniques rather than theory. After reading this book, you will be able to go into your groups and start doing things differently.

Reading this book will be helpful, but it is no substitution for hands-on training, supervision, and experience. There is an annual three-day advanced group therapy skills training workshop conducted near Chicago, Illinois.* This training explains and demonstrates the techniques described in this book and then gives participants the chance to practice the techniques and discuss problems and progress.

Not everyone can get to Chicago to attend this workshop, so a series of low-cost audio and video recordings of these workshops have been produced. These tapes make it possible for you to see the techniques as they are used in simulated group therapy sessions

---

* For information about the workshop entitled "Brief Strategic Problem-Solving Group Therapy" contact The CENAPS Corporation, 18650 Dixie Hwy, Homewood, IL 60430 (708/799-5000). Audio and video tapes of previous workshop sessions are available that include simulated group sessions that demonstrate and explain all the techniques described in this book. A list of professionals trained in these group methods is available. Just send a self-address stamped envelope to The CENAPS Corporation to become part of a growing international support group.

and hear the questions and reactions of people learning these methods. The CENAPS Corporation also maintains a list of professionals trained in these group methods.

The History of Problem-Solving Group Therapy

The brief strategic problem-solving group therapy method described in this book was first developed in the late 1960s. It was designed to guide patients systematically in solving specific target problems over a number of group sessions.

The techniques were based primarily on Adlerian psychotherapy principles that were adapted for use in treating chemically dependent patients. Over the years the problem-solving group techniques have been heavily influenced by the work of cognitive, behavioral, and experiential therapists.

I first learned an early version of this method from Richard Weedman at Grant Hospital of Chicago in 1969. He had learned the basic principles from Bob Postal, a psychotherapist teaching the technique through the Illinois Group Psychotherapy Association. I became fascinated with the method and have spent the last twenty-five years developing and refining its application to the treatment of chemical dependency and other behavioral health problems.

What the Problem-Solving Group Format Does

The problem-solving group format does several things. It rapidly establishes an effective group atmosphere that allows individual group members to work on different issues in the same session using a series of standard group process procedures. The standard format is designed to help the therapist track the implementation and completion of treatment techniques over a series of groups.

This problem-solving group format meets the needs of most MCOs because it targets specific problems, clearly defines treatment goals, and identifies specific time-limited interventions. Group members are systematically guided through each step of the intervention using powerful group techniques. Homework assignments and self-help groups are heavily integrated to accelerate the treatment process. Group members assume a high degree of ownership and responsibility for solving their own problems in collaboration with the group leader who guides them through a systematic problem-solving process. As a result problem-solving group therapy is preferred by the group members who have experienced it.

CHAPTER 2

An Introduction to Problem-Solving Group Therapy

This chapter will give you an overview of the basic principles and procedures that govern problem-solving group therapy. Group therapy will be defined and the four major goals of group therapy—changing how group members think, feel, act, and relate to people and situations—will be described. The role of structure and direction will be explained.

What Is Group Therapy?

Group therapy is a process of collective problem solving based on interpersonal involvement. A process is something that unfolds over time. A collective process involves more than one person working together. Problem solving means to identify and clarify a problem, find and evaluate alternative solutions, put those solutions to work, and evaluate the outcome. So problem-solving group therapy is the process of getting people to work together, over time, to solve problems by using systematic problem-solving methods.

The primary goal of problem-solving group therapy is to change how group members think, feel, act, and relate to others. We teach people to *change their thinking* by showing them new ways to define their problems and figure out solutions. We teach people to *change their feelings* by showing them how to identify and change the emotions they experience when thinking about or dealing with their problems. We teach people to *change their actions* by showing them how to break out of old self-defeating ways of behaving and start to do different things to solve their problems. We teach people how to *change their way of relating to others* by showing them new ways to involve other people in their personal problem solving.

The Four Goals of Problem-Solving Group Therapy

1. **Change in Thinking**: Teaching group members new ways to define their problems and figure out solutions.
2. **Change in Feeling**: Teaching group members how to identify and change the emotions they experience when thinking about their problems.
3. **Change in Actions**: Teaching group members to do something different to try and solve their problems.
4. **Change in Relating**: Teaching group members new ways to involve other people in personal problem solving.

Let's explore each of these goals in more depth.

Using Group to Change Irrational Thoughts

Problem-solving group therapy teaches the group members to change how they think by using a process called **cognitive restructuring**. The word *cognitive* means "information processing"; *restructuring* means "to structure or process in a new way." So cognitive restructuring means to change how people process information and ideas in their minds. This means teaching them to change their self-talk, mental images, and how they make judgments and decisions. In short, cognitive restructuring means changing how people think.

There are three cognitive restructuring techniques that will be used repeatedly in problem-solving groups: systematic problem solving, inner dialogue, and directive questioning. Let's briefly look at each of these techniques.

Systematic problem solving involves learning a proven three-step process for finding solutions to problems: problem identification and clarification; identifying alternatives and projecting logical consequences; and decision, action and evaluation. These three steps will be described in detail in a later chapter.

Inner dialogue techniques focus us on changing self-talk patterns. *Self-talk* involves the private conversations that people have with themselves. Most people have a rational side that thinks things through and makes decisions based on clear thinking and good common sense. Unfortunately, many people also have an irrational side that tells them to do things that are harmful or self-destructive.

In problem-solving group therapy, group members are taught to use these private conversations or inner dialogues to identify and resolve the conflicts between the rational, self-enhancing parts and the self-defeating parts of their personalities. Inner dialogues normally begin when people try to solve problems using a systematic process. Part of them says, "Go ahead, solve the problem!" Another part says, "Wait a minute! Why bother? This is too much work and isn't worth it!" By completing the inner dialogue process we can teach group members to overcome inner resistance that often prevents them from doing what they know they need to do to solve their problems.

Directive questioning is the third cognitive restructuring technique. Most people have a *private logic system* they use to make decisions and solve problems. Unfortunately, many times this private logic is flawed and actually creates more problems than it solves. Directive questioning is a technique that teaches people to become consciously aware of their private logic system, identify where that logic system is flawed or mistaken, and develop a new and more effective way of thinking about their problems.

The process of directive questioning involves asking an open-ended question (such as, "Why did you decide to start working at solving that problem today?"); paraphrasing the response ("What I'm hearing you say is ..."); and pointing out inconsistencies and asking the person to resolve them ("I'm confused because it seems like you are saying two different things. First you said..., and then you said.... I am having a hard time seeing how those two things relate to each other. Will you help me clarify this?").

These three techniques—systematic problem solving, inner dialogue, and directive questioning—when used together can promote a shift from irrational to rational ways of thinking.

Problem-solving groups also focus on teaching group members to change their thinking by using their imagination to solve their problems. The word *imagination* is built on the word *image*. An image is a picture that people develop in their minds. These pictures or images are based on the five senses: what we see, hear, touch, smell, and taste. When people consciously create pictures or images in their minds by imagining or trying to remember exactly what they saw, heard, touched, smelled, or tasted, they are creating **sensory images** or vivid pictures in their minds. Sometimes these images automatically come to mind. When this happens it is called **spontaneous imagery**. At other times people consciously have to create the image with the help of others. This is called **guided imagery**, because they are guided, directed, or helped to create the image by being asked to think about, remember, or imagine certain aspects of an experience.

Many people have never learned to control and direct these sensory images, memories, and fantasies. Because of this the images are vague, unfocused, and unregulated. In problem-solving groups the group leader teaches group members how to develop clear, focused, and self-regulated mental pictures and then use those mental pictures to solve problems. The techniques that do this are called **mental rehearsal techniques**. The goal of mental rehearsal is to use guided and spontaneous imagery to review and learn from past experiences and to develop and practice potential solutions to current problems. This allows group members to "try out" a solution in their minds before they actually put the solutions to work in the real world.

The Process of Changing How We Think

1. **Systematic Problem Solving**
   - Problem identification and clarification
   - Identifying alternatives and projecting logical consequences
   - Decision, action, and evaluation
2. **Inner Dialogue Techniques**
   - Identifying and resolving the internal arguments between the rational and irrational sides of our personalities
3. **Directive Questioning**
   - Allowing others to ask us questions that will force us to identify the steps in the private logic we use to solve our problems
4. **Mental Rehearsal**
   - Guided Imagery
   - Spontaneous Imagery

As group members learn to think logically and rationally by using inner dialogue and directive questioning techniques, then learn to create clear and focused imagery through guided imagery and mental rehearsal techniques, they begin improving their judgmental skills. **Good judgment is the ability to accurately and consistently predict the logical outcomes of behavior.** In group therapy many people experience a shift from the inability to accurately predict logical outcomes of behavior to the ability to do so.

The technique used to develop good judgment is the second step of systematic problem solving, which asks group members to identify alternative solutions to the problem and think about the logical consequence of each alternative. A logical consequence is what is most likely to happen if that alternative is used. This is often called *thinking a problem through before acting it out.*

With the development of good judgment, group members can begin to change or self-regulate their behaviors. In other words, they can start making choices about what they do or don't do based on the logical consequences of their behavior. Because behavior always has consequences, group members can start learning from the consequences of their behavior and make changes as their judgment and ability to regulate or control their behavior improves.

Using Group to Develop Emotional Management Skills

Problem-solving group therapy also teaches emotional management skills. Group members are taught to change how they manage their feelings by using a process of effective emotional management called **affective restructuring.** As group members work on solving problems they usually start to have feelings. Instead of ignoring these feelings, the group leader asks them to breathe deeply, notice the feelings and sensations, label them, and talk about them in the group. If they don't have words to describe what they are feeling, they will be taught a new emotional vocabulary so they can express what is going on inside of them.

The Process of Effective Emotional Management

1. **Recognition**—Learning to notice inner experiences. This often involves the use of spontaneous and guided imagery.
2. **Differentiation**—Learning to tell the difference between thoughts and feelings.
3. **Labeling**—Learning an emotional vocabulary that accurately describes your feelings.
4. **Communicating**—Telling others what you are feeling when it is safe to do so in a way that allows an empathetic response.

The first step of effective emotional management is **recognition.** Group members are encouraged to consciously monitor their inner experiences while in group and notice any changes or shifts. The next step is **differentiation** or learning to tell the difference between thoughts and feelings. Thinking occurs in the head and is regulated by logical thought processes. Feelings occur in the body and are regulated by imagery and sensory processes. Once group members know they are having thoughts and feelings, they can start talking about and accurately describing their thoughts and feelings in words. After **labeling** those thoughts and feelings, they can **communicate** their thoughts and feelings to others when it is appropriate to do so.

One way to help people identify the feelings that are caused by specific thoughts is to ask them to write down the thought statement and read it out loud while noticing their inner experiences. As they read the thought they are instructed to ask themselves, "What kind of feelings will be caused by thinking this thought?" They then construct a feeling statement that starts with the statement, "When I think this thought I tend to feel ...". The following list of feeling words can be used to help you describe feelings:

When I think this thought I tend to feel ...
1. strong and powerful
2. weak and helpless
3. angry, mad, or resentful
4. warm, caring, or protective
5. happy or joyful
6. sad, sorrowful, or depressed
7. safe, secure, or complacent
8. threatened, scared, or afraid
9. satisfield, fulfilled, or bored
10. stuck or frustrated
11. ashamed or guilty

The person reads the sentence stem, "When I think this thought I tend to feel ..." and completes it with each group of feeling words. The goal is to select the words that most closely describe what is being felt.

Using Group to Change Behavior

Problem-solving group therapy also teaches group members to change how they act or behave by using a process called **behavioral restructuring**. As they learn to self-regulate their behavior there is a shift from trying to control situations and the behavior of others to regulating their own reactions to the situations and people with which they interact. Group members learn to replace statements such as "You made me mad when you ..." with self-talk statements such as "I feel angry when I see you ...".

No one can control the situations they are in or the people they are with. The only thing they can control or regulate is their own behavior that they use to react to people and situations. Because of this, group therapy teaches people to identify **behavioral options** in response to problems. Group members learn how to do things that are good for them even though they don't want to. They are also taught how to resist urges or compulsions to do things that are harmful or self-destructive.

This process of behavioral restructuring can be described as a five-step process. The first step is to ***recognize self-defeating behaviors.*** Group members are taught the difference between a *self-enhancing behavior* (doing something that is good for them) and *self-defeating behavior* (doing something that is bad for them). At first this seems like a simple task, but on closer examination the problem is more difficult than it seems.

Group therapy teaches group members the difference between *immediate gratification* and *delayed gratification*. All behaviors have two sets of consequences: the immediate consequence (what happens to me right now when I do the behavior) and the long-term consequence (what happens to me later after I am done with the behavior).

Immediate gratification occurs when a behavior makes someone feel good right now. Some behaviors have immediate or instant gratification plus positive long-term consequences. These behaviors are ideal. They make people feel good now and enhance their lives later. As a result, most people are highly motivated to use them. Unfortunately, not all behaviors fall into this category.

The second category of behaviors includes those that make us feel bad right now *and* later. These behaviors are obviously self-defeating and few people feel an urge or compulsion to do them. If it hurts now and later, why bother? There is no payoff to provide motivation.

The third category of behaviors include those that make us feel good now, but hurt later. These behaviors often provide a powerful immediate gratification ("Wow! I love how this makes me feel!") but also produce negative, painful, or self-defeating long-term consequences ("It makes me hurt later"). These behaviors are often described as addictive, because in order to feel good now, many people are willing to pay the price of hurting later. They seek the short-term relief of using the addictive behavior again, which creates more pain in the future. They can continue this cycle until they have destroyed their lives.

The fourth category of behavior includes those that make us hurt or feel uncomfortable now, but cause us to feel good or experience benefits later. To gain these benefits people must learn to practice delayed gratification. In other words, they must be willing to hurt now in order to feel good later. This is the case in many responsible behaviors such as taking medication when sick, exercising, or keeping to a healthful meal plan. The problem here is to learn how to overcome the natural resistance to the immediate pain or discomfort by keeping the focus on the long-term benefit. People need discipline to engage in the difficult behavior and faith that the long-term benefit will follow.

Many people make the mistake of confusing the immediate good feeling with judging the behavior as self-enhancing. Unfortunately, as we discussed, many things that produce an immediate good feeling, such as using alcohol and drugs, can have very destructive long-term consequences. Other behaviors that produce immediate uncomfortable feelings, such as exercising and eating right, can produce very positive long-term consequences.

Many self-defeating behaviors make us feel good now and cause us to hurt later. People are drawn to the immediate gratification even though they know the behaviors will hurt them in the long run. This is the basis of most addictive and compulsive disorders. In group therapy individuals start learning the skill of delayed gratification. They learn how to recognize self-defeating urges and to say no. This process is often called *impulse control*. They also learn how to recognize the long-term negative consequence ("If I do it, it will hurt me in the long run") and how to resist the urge ("No, I won't act out this behavior now").

The second step in behavioral restructuring is *identifying self-enhancing alternative behaviors*. It is not enough to stop doing something; people must learn to do something else instead. This often involves replacing immediate gratification (behaviors that make us feel good now but hurt us later) with self-enhancing behaviors. Unfortunately, many self-enhancing behaviors require us to do things that make us feel uncomfortable now to feel better later.

The third step in behavioral restructuring is to *resist the urge to act out self-defeating behavior*. Group members have to learn how to say no when they feel the urge to say yes. Often this involves support, encouragement, and sometimes confrontation from others. This is where therapy group comes into play. With permission, other group members confront group members who are having urges to act out on self-defeating behavior and provide feedback, encouragement, and confrontation to help them overcome the urge to fall back into self-defeating behaviors that will hurt them in the long run.

The fourth step in behavioral restructuring is to *overcome resistance to using self-enhancing behaviors*. As mentioned before, people have to start doing self-enhancing things to change. This often feels uncomfortable and sometimes it is outright painful. Group members have to learn to feel the fear and the pain and do what they need to do anyway. This is the essence of *courage*—the ability to face fear and pain and to do what needs to be done anyway. Again, group therapy can provide the motivation and support to help accomplish this.

Behavioral Restructuring

1. Recognize self-defeating behaviors.
2. Identify self-enhancing alternative behaviors.
3. Resist the urge to act out self-defeating behavior.
4. Overcome resistance to using self-enhancing behaviors.
5. Practice self-enhancing behaviors until they become habitual.

The good news is that if people practice self-enhancing behaviors long enough, the pain goes away and the behaviors begin to feel natural. This process takes about six weeks. So the fifth step of behavioral restructuring is to **practice self-enhancing behaviors until they become habitual.** To accomplish this, group members generally stay in group for ten to twelve weeks.

Using Group to Change Relationships with People and Situations

Group therapy teaches people how to relate to people and situations in a more positive and proactive manner. Because this process involves changing or restructuring relationships, it is called **social restructuring**. Group members learn how to manage their relationships better by improving their communication skills, learning to work cooperatively with others, and practicing rigorous but respectful honesty with other people.

A primary step of social restructuring is to identify the people who enable self-defeating behaviors. As we discussed earlier, because many self-defeating behaviors feel good, people mistakenly believe these behaviors are good for them. As a result they tend to feel bad about anyone or anything that challenges their use of these behaviors. They also may feel that people who point out their problem behaviors and the pain they cause are being critical or unfair.

This first thing group members need to learn is that healthy people who love and care about them won't sit quietly by while they hurt themselves and destroy their lives. Healthy people usually confront their friends and family members when they see them lapse into self-defeating behavior. This type of confrontation makes the people who receive it feel uncomfortable.

Many times they respond by pushing the people who are giving the confrontation out of their lives or by manipulating them into shutting up and leaving them alone. The people who are manipulated can become **enablers**. They silently watch the people they love destroy themselves because they don't want to create hard feelings by telling them what they see them doing that is setting themselves up for pain and problems. At times enablers will actively participate in and encourage the self-destructive behaviors of friends and family just to avoid making them feel upset or bad about them.

For individuals to make permanent changes they must *identify* the people and situations that enable them in their self-defeating behaviors, *expose* the enabling behaviors, and *work* with them to change how they respond to problematic behavior. The goal is to teach other people how to support their self-enhancing behaviors while confronting or refusing to support their self-defeating behaviors.

Types of Group Therapy

The goal of changing thoughts, feelings, behaviors, and relationships can be accomplished with several different types of groups. Four common group formats are used: psychoeducation groups, discussion groups, experiential groups, and problem-solving groups.

Types of Groups

1. Psychoeducation Groups
2. Discussion Groups
3. Experiential Groups
4. Problem-Solving Groups

Psychoeducation groups are didactic or teaching groups. The goal is to present new information to group members and guide them through exercises or group processes that allow them to personalize that information. Psychoeducation groups are heavily structured, and all group members work on the same issues in accordance with a standard agenda. This standardization is both the biggest strength and the biggest weakness of psychoeducation groups. If group members are carefully selected based on their need to participate in the structured program, they can gain tremendous benefits. The problem is that there is a limited ability to adapt or adjust the psychoeducational group process to meet the individual needs of group members who don't fit into the standard agenda.

Discussion groups are designed for sharing information and opinions. Generally there is a topic selected and participants are encouraged to discuss their reactions to the topics. Once again, all group members focus on the topic rather than the individual needs of group members. Although there is usually more flexibility in a discussion group, there are limits to how far the group can move from the topic of day. As a result, group members who do not have problems with the general topic gain minimal benefits.

Experiential groups are designed for feeling identification, feeling resolution, and communication training. The primary focus is the immediate here-and-now interactions of group members. The goal is to create intense experiences within the session and use those experiences as a therapeutic springboard for self-examination and change. The strength of experiential groups is that they help people connect with, express, and resolve feelings and emotions. A weakness is that there is often a lack of opportunity to understand how the experiences in the group can be applied to solving problems or making changes outside of the group.

The final type, **problem-solving groups**, is designed to identify and solve the individual problems of group members. This book is designed to describe, in depth, the techniques and procedures used in problem-solving groups. The other types of groups are valuable and have a definite place in treatment programs. It is beyond the scope of this book, however, to describe these other group formats and their use in detail.

The Elements of Effective Problem-solving Groups

Effective problem-solving groups are structured, directive, consistent, problem focused, disorder specific, and supportive. Let's explore each term in more detail.

Effective group therapy is...

- **Structured:**
  Uses a standard agenda
- **Directive:**
  Clearly defines and enforces expectations
- **Consistent:**
  Follows standard rules and responsibilities
- **Problem focused:**
  Identifies and resolves target problems
- **Disorder specific:**
  Works on issues related to the diagnosed disorder
- **Supportive:**
  Supports the person while pointing out self-defeating ways of thinking and behaving

---

Problem-solving groups are **structured**. They use a standard group agenda that defines consistent rules, roles, and rituals. *Rules* define what the group members can and cannot not do during the group. *Roles* describe the type of behavior that is appropriate or inappropriate. *Rituals* are group procedures that force group members to practice specific forms of responsible behavior over and over again until they become deeply ingrained habits.

Problem-solving groups are **directive**. This means that expectations are clearly defined and enforced. All group members are expected to have identified problems related to their target disorder that they are willing to work on in group. They are expected to use a standard problem-solving process to work at resolving those problems. They are also given homework assignments that they are expected to complete. This direction provides a context for growth and change.

Problem-solving groups are **consistent**. There are routine rules, processes, and group skills used repeatedly. This creates familiarity and a sense of safety. Group members know what to expect. There are specific skills they can learn that allow them to function well and get results as a group member.

Problem-solving groups are **problem focused**. The goal is to solve the target problem that is the reason for the group member to be attending group sessions. This doesn't mean that all the work is intellectual. Good problem-solving groups integrate all domains of functioning—thinking, feeling, behaviors, and relationship styles—in the group problem-solving process. Most group members tend to act out the problems they are trying to solve in the group. By exposing and giving feedback to group members about these here-and-now behaviors that are part of the problem, a sense of immediacy and intense experience is created.

Problem-solving groups are **disorder specific**. As mentioned earlier, efforts are made to match group members based on both diagnosis and stage of recovery. This creates a sense of commonality that allows group members to identify easily with one another and accelerate the group bonding process.

Problem-solving groups are **supportive**. A primary goal of problem-solving groups is to create an environment of safety and honesty in which problems can be identified and resolved. This is done by *separating the person from the problem*. The group supports each member as a person while pointing out self-defeating behaviors.

Group Rules, Roles, and Rituals

Group rules clearly define what group members can or cannot do in the group. This creates *safety*. When group members feel safe because they know what to expect and what is going to happen, they become willing to take risks by talking about things they normally would keep secret. This allows them to start dealing with problems they previously have been unable to talk about.

The Roles Group Members Play

1. Talk and present problems
2. Respond to directive questioning
3. Listen when others present problems
4. Ask directive questions to help others solve problems
5. Give feedback
6. Receive feedback

The **roles** people play in group allow them to change how they behave. At times group members *talk and present problems*. Then they shift roles and learn how to *listen and respond*. At times they take on the role of a *curious questioner* trying to help other group members understand their problems in a new way. At other times they *allow themselves to be questioned* by other group members trying to answer as honestly and completely as they can in order to think about or view their problems in new, more helpful ways. Group members also *give feedback* to one another by telling them what they think their problem is and how they feel about them as a person. Group members also *receive feedback* from other group members about their problems and behavior.

Group rituals are things that group members do over and over again. There are many ritualized behaviors in the group. Every session opens with a ritual called **reactions to last session** in which each group member reports what he or she thought and felt about the last group, and identifies three people who stood out to them and why. This ritual helps get the group started quickly and efficiently. It also helps each group member, including the group leader, to remember what happened in the last group and gets them ready to discuss their problems openly and honestly.

During the problem-solving portion of group, a problem-solving ritual is used. A group member volunteers to present a problem or issue while the other group members ask clarifying questions, give feedback, and help the person find an assignment to move on to the next step of problem solving.

Every session ends with a ritual called the **closure exercise** in which group members take the time to discuss the most important thing they learned in group and what they plan to do differently as a result of what they learned. This helps them make sense out of the group, set up clear action plans to get ready for the next group, and use what they learned in between group sessions.

CHAPTER 3

Problem-Solving Group Therapy and Other Modalities

Problem-solving group therapy is usually the central modality or method of treatment. The problem-solving group provides coordination with other treatment modalities, tracks the completion of therapeutic assignments, measures progress, and identifies and resolves problems. It is also ideal because it allows a single group leader to work with a larger number of clients and provides for peer group support and confrontation that cannot occur in individual therapy.

Building a Structured Recovery Program

Although group therapy is central to the recovery process for many people with chemical dependency and other behavioral health problems, group therapy alone often is not enough. For group therapy to be truly effective it must be integrated with four other vital components: a structured recovery program, a long-term therapeutic relationship, consistent peer group support, and a program of holistic health care.

People recovering from chemical dependency or other behavioral health problems often have lives that are centered on their target problem behaviors. When these self-defeating activities are removed, the basic core organizing activities are taken out of their lives. They must be replaced with something more positive or the recovering people will relapse.

Group Therapy Must Be Integrated with ...

1. a structured recovery program;
2. a long-term therapeutic relationship;
3. consistent peer group support; and
4. a program of holistic health care.

The primary tool for providing group members with a basic life structure is called a **structured recovery program.** An effective recovery program consists of a regular schedule of activities designed to promote stable and responsible living. It also provides a foundation from which to intervene should relapse warning signs develop or a group member relapses to the use of the target behavior.

The recovery program provides a consistent schedule of activities. The less structured the group member's life, the more recovery activities that will be needed to structure it. Unemployed group members with no stable family unit will require a supervised living program in a halfway house. More stable group members may work in supervised living programs where they work during the day, attend therapy and self-help activities in the evening, and return to the supervised facility to sleep and for morning check-in. Other group members may work a regular job and attend recovery activities during the evening and on weekends.

A typical recovery program combines five treatment modalities: group therapy, individual therapy, recovery education, family therapy, and self-help group involvement.

Recovery Program Components

1. Group Therapy
2. Individual Therapy
3. Recovery Education
4. Family Therapy
5. Self-help Groups

Group Therapy

Group therapy is the core component of treatment. Through involvement in a problem-solving group, recovering group members learn basic communication and problem-solving skills. They learn how to follow a structured group format, identify and solve problems, and work effectively with other group members. They also learn how to view structure as a means of getting free from self-defeating behaviors and the personality traits that drive them.

Individual Therapy

Individual therapy is designed to support involvement in the problem-solving group. It is in individual sessions that group members learn how to build a positive relationship with a sober and responsible person—the individual therapist. It is best for group members to have an individual therapist who is either the leader or coleader of their group. In this way individual therapy can be designed to support the identification and resolution of problems within the group.

Recovery Education

Recovery education consists of structured classes that teach the group member the basics about their target disorder, the recovery process, recovery resources, and how to access them. Recovery education sessions provide straightforward, no-nonsense classes that teach practical information and skills needed for recovery.

The recovery education sessions are structured and include a *pretest* that measures the basic knowledge the group member brings into the session. This is followed by a twenty- to thirty-minute lecture. An *educational exercise* is then used to involve participants in using the information that is presented. This is followed by a *discussion* of what was learned during the lecture and exercise. The session ends with a *posttest* that measures what was learned during the session.[a]

Participants are held accountable for what they learn. The pre- and posttest are scored, and if the group member has low scores on the posttest he or she is expected to take the session over. The level of participation in educational exercises is monitored, and the participant's ability to apply the information to their own life circumstances is monitored during the discussion periods.

Family Therapy

Family therapy is an important component because most group members live in a family system. Group members usually have ongoing relationships with parents and siblings, spouses or lovers, and frequently children, often from a variety of marriages or relationships. As a result the concept of family therapy needs to be expanded to include these multiple dimensions. Research indicates that appropriate involvement of family members in the group members' recovery program can lower relapse rates.

Self-help Groups

Self-help groups, such as Alcoholics Anonymous (AA), Narcotics Anonymous (NA), and other Twelve Step programs are a vital component in the group member's recovery plan.[b] It is through self-

---

a. The book *Recovery Education: A Guide for Teaching Chemically Dependent People* by Merlene Miller provides an excellent overview of the use of adult learning principles in teaching chemically dependent patients about their disease and recovery. Copies are available from Herald House/Independence Press.

b. The book *Understanding the Twelve Steps* by Terence T. Gorski provides an interpretation of Twelve Step principles that is compatible with the cognitive behavioral principles used in problem-solving group therapy. Copies are available from Herald House/Independence Press.

help group involvement that group members begin to expand their recovery program into voluntary and loosely monitored activities. This begins a vital transition from externally imposed and monitored treatment to treatment involvement that is voluntary and self-regulated.

Self-help groups are a critical part of recovery and should be a mandatory part of the recovery program. Twelve Step programs such as Alcoholics Anonymous (AA) and Narcotics Anonymous (NA) have been enormously successful in criminal justice settings.* For people in dual recovery (chemical dependency and related personality or mental disorders), involvement in MICA groups or Dual Recovery Anonymous is helpful. Getting group members actively involved in Twelve Step programs can increase recovery and lower relapse rates. It is recommended that group members attend a minimum of three self-help meetings each week throughout their supervised recovery period.

A Long-Term Therapeutic Relationship

Many people entering problem-solving group therapy have never had a long-term, one-on-one relationship with a sober and responsible adult. Such a relationship provides role modeling, relationship training, and directed positive and negative feedback. This relationship is provided primarily through consistent individual therapy and can be crucial to a group member's recovery. A long-term individual relationship can also occur in Twelve Step programs by encouraging the recovering person to find a sponsor who can teach them about the program and be available for private conversations on a regular basis to help them through the rough times of recovery.

Role modeling occurs as group members meet regularly with the same counselor or therapist. They get to see firsthand how the coun-

---

* The three-part series by Terence T. Gorski, *Relapse Prevention Therapy with Chemically Dependent Criminal Offenders* (available from Herald House/Independence Press) provides an excellent introduction to this expanding field. The three books are: *An Executive Briefing for Judges and Policymakers* (Part 1); *A Guide for Counselors, Therapists, and Criminal Justice Professionals* (Part 2); and *The Relapse Prevention Workbook for the Criminal Offender* (Part 3).

selor deals with them and how they handle problems. **Relationship training** occurs as group members learn how to bond with another human being and how to use basic interpersonal skills. By talking about resolving issues and dealing with the feelings that come up in the course of the relationship, the group member can learn how to develop a primary relationship in a healthy way through direct experience. There is no replacement for this immediate experience with a socially responsible adult.

In the context of individual therapy, group members can receive consistent, directed, positive and negative feedback from a socially responsible adult with whom they have developed a trusting relationship. The group member becomes psychologically visible through this feedback and begins to learn how other responsible people perceive his or her strengths and weaknesses. This new point of view gives an opportunity to change and a point to compare the feedback from their counselor (a responsible person) with that from their peers.

Consistent Peer Group Support

Recovering group members need to replace peer relationships that are centered on target behaviors with relationships centered on recovery. This means getting involved with other responsible people. The process begins in the group therapy programs and is carried forward in self-help groups, and it eventually leads to developing friendships and sober, responsible networks of friends outside of the treatment context.

Consistent peer feedback is provided in problem-solving group therapy and through involvement in self-help programs. This feedback breaks the pattern of social isolation and allows the group member to feel connected with other people and develop social interest. Group members have to attend the same group and interact with the same people consistently. They must deal with the long-term impact of their behaviors on others. They can't simply leave when the going gets rough.

The group also provides an experimental laboratory to try out new behaviors. The group member can act in new and different ways within the group to see what happens by experimenting in a safe environment. The peer group also reinforces responsible behavior patterns while providing a source of "credible" confrontation. There is a saying that goes "You can't con a con." In group therapy members become visible to themselves through the minds and hearts of other group members. They tend to respect the feedback they get from their peers because they feel it is honest and being provided by people who know where they are coming from.

A Program of Holistic Health Care

A holistic health program involves activities that group members complete to stay healthy, manage stress, and resolve conflicts on a daily basis. These activities are often done alone and include such things as a healthful diet, proper exercise, stress management, recreation and relaxation, and a spiritual program of recovery.

Because group and individual therapy are so important to ongoing recovery, the next chapter will look in depth at how to conduct a successful program of group and individual therapy.

CHAPTER 4

The Administrative Aspects of Problem-Solving Group Therapy

Group leaders often have problems because they have not properly understood the importance of the administrative aspects of group therapy. A successful group therapy program requires effective policies and procedures that are developed and supported by top management in the treatment program. These policies and procedures need to govern such things as group leadership, the credentials of group leaders, group size, duration of group sessions, group rules and responsibilities, and corrective discipline for non-compliant group members.

An important issue is defining group responsibilities, rules, and a standard agenda for use by all therapists within the program. This allows better cooperation and communication among clinical staff while providing consistency if patients transfer from one group to another or if different therapists need to temporarily run a group due to illness or vacation.

Let's review the most common administrative issues that affect the clinical functioning of problem-solving therapy groups.

Classifying and Matching Group Members

Many group problems occur because group members are not appropriately matched. With proper matching, group members will have higher levels of peer identification and are more willing to become involved in the group process. When not properly matched, group members often feel like they don't belong. As a result they become reluctant to discuss their problems ("Everyone here is so different they won't understand me!"), listen to feedback ("What can someone like that possibly know that could help me?"), or try to help others solve their problems ("This person is so different from me, I don't know how to help them!"). One way of appropriately matching patients is to develop admission and discharge criteria for each group.

There are two useful methods for classifying group members using criteria based on diagnosis or stage of recovery.

Matching Group Members by Diagnosis

In early recovery it is best to assign people to groups with others who share the same diagnosis. Chemically dependent patients, for example, tend to do better in groups with other chemically dependent people. The same is true of people suffering from depressive illness, post traumatic stress disorder, schizophrenia, or other behavioral health problems. All group members share the common experience of trying to cope with the symptoms of their illness. The treatment strategies used to help each group member will also be similar so group members can learn about managing their own behavioral health problems by assisting other members of the group.

When groups consist of people with a wide range of behavioral health disorders, group cohesion tends to become a problem. Group members have a difficult time identifying with one another. They have a greater tendency to "compare out" by saying to themselves that they have nothing in common with other group members. When this happens they can easily come to the conclusion that the group can't help them or that no one will understand their problems. When this occurs they are likely to drop out quickly.

Matching Group Members by Stage of Recovery

Classifying group members by stage of recovery is helpful. In the book *Passages Through Recovery: An Action Plan for Preventing Relapse*,[a] I describe a six-stage developmental model of recovery. Although this model was originally developed for use with chemically dependent patients,[b] the stages compare favorably with general research on the stages of change.[c] As a result this model is being used successfully to describe the recovery process from a variety of chronic, lifestyle-related behavioral health disorders ranging from post traumatic stress disorder to eating disorders.

The Developmental Model of Recovery suggests that there are six progressive stages of recovery from most target disorders. The first stage is a **transition** stage where people have high levels of denial and treatment resistance. They don't recognize or accept that they have the target disorder, and external circumstances intervene to force them into treatment. *Motivational groups* that focus primarily on breaking denial, overcoming resistance, and educating about the target disorder are most effective for patients in this stage of recovery.

The second stage of recovery is **stabilization** where people are recovering from the medical illness, debilitating stress, and psychosocial crisis caused by the target disorder. In this stage people are usually unstable, volatile, and having difficulty controlling their behavior and functioning normally. Some patients are so dysfunctional they are not appropriate group candidates. People in the stabilization stage of recovery can benefit from *symptom management groups* that focus on identifying and managing the immediate

---

a. *Passages Through Recovery* by Terence T. Gorski is available from Herald House/Independence Press.

b. Another excellent book describing a developmental model of recovery from chemical dependency is *Treating the Alcoholic: A Developmental Model* by Stephanie Brown (New York: John Wiley and Sons, 1985).

c. The book *Changing for Good: The Revolutionary Program that Explains the Six Stages of Change and Teaches You How to Free Yourself from Bad Habits* by James O. Prochaska, John C. Norcross, and Carlo C. DiClimente describes a general model for changing behavior that is widely accepted.

crisis and severe symptoms that are interfering with normal functioning.

The third stage is **early recovery** where people recognize and become willing to recover but lack knowledge about their target disorder and how to recover. They are generally well motivated and willing to follow advice and recommendations. People in early recovery can benefit from *primary recovery groups* that teach them about their target disorder and help them identify and change the thoughts, feelings, behaviors, and relationship styles related to that disorder. They can also benefit from using the group to reinforce attendance at psychoeducational groups and the development of a community-based recovery program including self-help groups and other low-cost community resources to reinforce the work done in group therapy.

The fourth stage is **middle recovery** where people have changed the thinking, feelings, and behaviors directly related to their target disorder. They have not yet identified or changed the enabling relationships and situations in their life that support their target disorder. People in middle recovery generally do well in primary recovery groups with people in the early stage of recovery. This is because it is difficult to focus on the internal changes of early recovery without exploring how those changes are impacting other people and relationships.

The fifth stage is **late recovery** where people are working on deep changes in their values and personality that are necessary to continued growth and development and to avoid relapse. These patients are often working on family-of-origin issues and related issues of psychological growth. People in late recovery do best in separate *advanced recovery groups or psychotherapy groups.*

Matching Groups by Stage of Recovery

Stage of Recovery	Primary Goal	Type of Group
Transition	Interrupt denial and resistance	Motivational Counseling Groups
Stabilization	Regain control over thoughts, feelings, and behaviors	Symptom Management Groups
Early Recovery	Changing the irrational thoughts, unmanageable feelings, and self-defeating behaviors that drive the target disorder	Basic Recovery Groups
Middle Recovery	Interrupting enabling relationships, lifestyle repair, and lifestyle balance	Basic Recovery Groups
Late Recovery	Deep personality and value change	Psychotherapy Groups
Maintenance	Continued growth and development	Personal Growth Groups
Relapse	Identification and management of relapse warning signs	Relapse Prevention Groups

The final stage of recovery is **maintenance**. During this stage clients are leading a normal life, working a holistic recovery program, continuing with personal growth and development, and watching for and managing relapse warning signs. These people are normally functioning with self-help groups and periodic follow-up sessions.

Many patients will relapse as they progress through these stages of recovery. At times, these relapses can be stabilized and patients can successfully recover by returning to the same group they were in when the relapse occurred. At other times, especially with chronic relapsers who have long-term and destructive relapses, it is helpful to place them in separate *relapse prevention groups* with other relapsers. These groups focus exclusively upon the issue of identifying and managing relapse warning signs.

Group as an Experimental Laboratory for Behavioral Change

Problem-solving groups are best viewed as experimental laboratories in which clients can try out new behaviors and see what happens. Groups should be structured to provide a safe, consistent environment. While it is important to point out self-defeating behaviors and their consequences, research has shown that harsh confrontation that tears down defenses and attacks the basic integrity of group members actually lowers self-esteem and raises the risk of relapse.

It is therefore recommended that group therapy should be structured, directive, and supportive. **Structured groups** follow a standard agenda and allow all group members to know what procedures are going to be followed. It allows them to get comfortable with the group process and master the skills needed to be an effective group member. **Directive groups** expect group members to follow certain procedures. They are told or directed to comply with certain basic rules, responsibilities, and procedures. They are told how to behave, what to do, and are expected to fulfill the behavioral expectations. **Supportive groups** seek to find the positive characteristics and behaviors of group members and to reinforce them.

In supportive group therapy the individual is separated from the self-defeating behavior. This approach is captured in the statement commonly used in giving feedback: *"I can't understand why an intelligent person like you who wants to solve this problem would use such self-defeating behavior! Can we look at what you did, what motivated you to do it, and what you could do differently in the future?"*

Effective Group Therapy Is ...

1. Structured
2. Directive
3. Supportive

Notice how this approach supports the individual by assuming there is a healthy, motivated person who wants to recover. It doesn't enable or ignore the self-defeating behavior. It directly says, "You are doing things that are hurting you instead of helping you," and then invites the group member to look at new, more constructive ways of approaching the problems.

Group Leadership

Problem-solving groups are usually led by a single therapist or a two-person therapy team. The two-person therapy team consists of a **group leader**, who is responsible for the group, and a **coleader**, who assists the group leader in leading the group and documenting progress and problems. Group leaders can be trained in a variety of disciplines and can include psychologists, social workers, professional counselors, alcohol and drug abuse counselors, and other helping professionals.

No matter what the professional credentials, it is important that group leaders be trained in problem-solving group therapy methods that support the identification and resolution of problems related to resolving the target problem and promoting ongoing improvements in biopsychosocial health.

It is preferable to have two professionals in the group to avoid manipulation by group members. Many group members have deeply entrenched mistaken beliefs and self-defeating or manipulative coping styles. Unless the group leader has another professional in the group, it is easy to lose perspective and get sucked into the clients' denial and manipulation systems.

It is not always fiscally possible to have two paid therapists in the group. Many programs use trained volunteers or interns from a local college or university to fill the coleader position. This provides another person for reality testing without exceeding budget requirements.

Roles Played by the Group Therapist

Group leaders play many different roles in the group. As **group leader** they establish and enforce the rules, responsibilities, and corrective procedures. As **teacher** they explain and demonstrate the skills group members need to learn. As **coach** they carefully watch how group members perform and give feedback and encouragement in the use of new skills and behaviors. As **case manager** they help coordinate the group process with other treatment modalities. As **problem solver** they guide the group members through the use of a standard problem-solving procedure.

An effective group leader will be able to shift roles easily and spontaneously to meet emerging needs of the group. By keeping these roles clearly in mind, the group leader can make decisions about which role is appropriate in response to different situations that occur in group.

The Three P's of Group

An effective group leader provides good, orderly direction for the group process by practicing the "Three P's of Group Therapy": permission, protection, and potency. Group leaders give group members **permission** to experiment with new ways of thinking and acting in group. As group members move out of their comfort zone by experimenting, the group leaders provide **protection** by assuring that the group is a safe environment in which to experiment. They are willing to set and enforce consistent rules and confront the inappropriate or dangerous behaviors of other group members. The group leaders have **potency**. In other words, they are willing and able to exercise their authority—and all the group members know it.

As a result group leaders become the keeper of the group process. They set the pace and the timing for various group procedures. They work collaboratively with group members in assigning and monitoring the completion of homework assignments. They identify and resolve group problems.

The group leader becomes a powerful role model for group members. The general rule of role modeling is this: *If you expect it from group members, you had better be able to do it yourself.* This role-modeling expectation is what makes functioning as a group leader so exciting and challenging. As a group leader you have to master and consistently utilize all the techniques and procedures that you expect your group members to learn and use.

Group Size

Effective problem-solving groups usually have between six and ten group members. It is important to limit the size of problem-solving groups to assure that all group members have time to work on their problems. The larger the group, the less intense the experience will be for all members. At somewhere between ten and twelve members, a group stops being a group and starts being an audience. At this point genuine interpersonal problem solving is inhibited and only the most extroverted clients are comfortable presenting problems.

At somewhere between ten and twelve members, a group stops being a group and starts being an audience.

Because problem-solving groups are not effective with more than twelve people, other forms of group therapy are suggested if larger groups are needed. Such group formats include lecture and discussion, fish-bowl techniques that work with a small group of selected members while other group members observe, or working with one group member while others observe and ask questions. It is beyond the scope of this book to describe these other types of group therapy in detail.

Duration of Group Sessions

Problem-solving groups generally last between one-and-a-half and three hours, with a two-hour group being the most common. Groups that are shorter than one-and-a-half hours generally are ineffective because there is not enough time to work on issues in depth. By the time the group is warmed up and ready to work, the session is over. In shorter groups only one or two group members get to work in each group. This means that most members have long gaps between presenting their problems to the group, and this can slow down problem solving. Groups that are longer than three hours tend to be ineffective because group members become tired and stressed and begin to shut down.

To keep group members actively involved in the problem-solving process there must be clearly stated and enforced group responsibilities and rules, as well as a standard group agenda. They learn about these responsibilities, rules, and agenda in an orientation session.

Orientation of New Group Members

It is important to meet with new group members before they begin the group. The purpose of this initial meeting is to: identify and clarify the problems to be worked on in group; determine that the client is appropriate for the group; assure that the client will relate well with other group members; explain the rules and responsibilities of group members; introduce the standard problem-solving group therapy agenda; and secure a group participation contract.

It is important that new group members understand and verbally agree to comply with these rules and responsibilities. The time to engage in a power struggle is in an individual session *before* the new member enters group. If the group member resists entering the group, the time to use therapeutic leverage and threaten consequences is up front, in private, before the client enters the group. This saves a lot of group time and avoids unnecessary confrontation and an adverse climate setting in the group.

Dealing with Resistant Clients

Clients frequently will resist becoming involved in group therapy initially because they feel threatened or exposed. It is important to insist on group involvement for most people with chemical dependency and other behavioral health problems. Group therapy can provide opportunities for communication training, problem solving, and positive peer pressure that are essential for recovery.

Using Individual Therapy to Support the Group Process

Experience with problem-solving group therapy shows that groups run more efficiently and effectively when group members have individual sessions that are designed to support the ongoing group process. This is especially true when group members are strongly resistant, exhibit high levels of denial, or have difficulty learning from past experience or maintaining a consistent direction in solving a problem. Because people with chemical dependency and other behavioral health problems fit all these characteristics, it is important to conduct individual sessions that support the ongoing problem-solving group process.

Group members are more likely to comply with established group procedures if they have met one or more times with the group leader before entering the group. This allows the group leader to establish his or her authority, explain the problem-solving group process, and establish a clear contract for participation. The group contract should be based on clearly identified problem issues related to the target problem. A step-by-step plan should be created that will be used to solve those problems. Group members must believe that being in group can help them deal with some problem that is troubling them. This process of identifying the initial problems and proposing ways the group can help to solve them motivates the problem solver and lowers resistance during the first several groups.

A primary goal of individual therapy is to provide a consistent one-to-one therapeutic relationship with the group member. It is important to remember the group leader may be one of the few responsible problem solvers the group member has ever had a close personal relationship with. If the group member can interact in a positive way with the group leader and accept the group leader as a role model, problem solving will progress far more rapidly. Spending time with group members in carefully planned individual sessions allows this bonding process to occur more quickly, and it generally makes the group member more receptive to working productively in the group and far less likely to sabotage the work of other group members.

Standard Agenda for Individual Therapy

There is a recommended standard agenda for individual sessions that includes the following: reactions to last session, a recovery check, assignment review, group preparation, and topic-oriented conversation. Let's look at each item on this agenda.

Agenda for Individual Therapy
1. Reactions to Last Session
2. Recovery Check
3. Assignment Review
4. Group Preparation
5. Topic-Oriented Conversation

Reactions to Last Session

This procedure is similar to the reactions presented in group. Group members are asked what they thought about their last individual and group session, how they felt about the last session, and what they have been doing differently as result of the therapy they have been receiving. This procedure focuses group members on doing something different and on positive change in between sessions as a primary goal of recovery.

Recovery Check

The therapist leads the group member through a recovery check that involves asking the client to answer the following questions:

- Have you relapsed to the use of your target problem behavior since our last session?
- Have you had the urge or compulsion to use your target problem behavior since your last group or individual session?
- Have you attended all of the scheduled activities on your recovery plan?
- Have you experienced any resistance or resentments about maintaining your recovery plan?

This recovery check allows the counselors to quickly identify any serious relapse warning signs that may threaten the group members' ongoing recovery. It also keeps the focus clearly on doing what is necessary to avoid relapsing into the use of the target problem behaviors.

Assignment Review

The next part of the session is devoted to an assignment review. This is completed by asking what assignment is being worked on and the problems and progress the client is experiencing while working on it. Because the assignment is directly related to solving the target problem, this procedure keeps a clear problem focus. If the group member is not working on an assignment or doesn't remember what it is, this becomes a critical issue.

Group Preparation

The next part of the session is devoted to group preparation. The therapist works with the group member to develop a plan for presenting the issue in group. This also involves instruction and practice in basic group skills such as how to give a reaction, how to do active listening, how to ask an open-ended question, how to give feedback, and how to do the closure exercise. This group preparation should be based on a skill-building philosophy. Group members must learn the skills needed to carry out their responsibilities in group. The individual session can help them build those skills.

Topic-Oriented Conversation

For group members who are actively involved in their recovery, the individual session is devoted entirely to reactions, the recovery check, assignment review, and group preparation. Resistant group members, however, often have little to say about these things. As a result, the therapist should always be prepared with topic-oriented conversation to use should the group member have nothing else to work on. These topics can cover broad areas such as recognition and acceptance of the target problem, how it feels to comply with a recovery program, denial and resistance, or personality traits and lifestyle patterns that support the target problem behavior. The topics should be selected to match issues that are being experienced by the group member.

CHAPTER 5

Documentation

Documentation is an important part of group therapy, especially in the era of cost containment. Managed care organizations and other third-party payers need to see a clear justification for people being in group therapy, a target problem the group is working on, a goal for resolution of the target problem, and a step-by-step action plan for solving the problem. To do this the group therapist needs a system for dealing with treatment planning and documentation. Here are my suggestions.

Brief Strategic Assessment

Before starting anyone in group therapy have an individual session with them. In this session clearly identify the **target treatment problem** that will be the central focus of the group therapy effort. Take a **target problem history** showing when the person first experienced the problem, what he or she has done to try and solve the problem, and what has and has not been helpful. Set an **outcome goal** by discussing with the person what his or her life will look like when the problem is resolved. Be concrete and specific.

Develop an **action plan** or a series of interventions that lead logically to the resolution of the problem. This action plan should be based on some method of systematic problem solving and should incorporate the identification and change of the irrational thoughts, unmanageable feelings, and self-defeating behaviors and relationships that drive the target problem.

Link each step of the action plan to a group therapy activity, homework assignment, or individual therapy session. This is vital. Each action step must describe where and how it will be accomplished. The entire sequence of problem resolution steps needs to be conceptualized up front. There will be opportunities to adjust or modify strategies, but the group member should buy into the general steps of the action plan.

The Group Therapy Attendance Binder

The biggest single obstacle to effective documentation of group sessions is access to the charts. In surveys I have completed in group therapy training sessions, more than half of the participants reported they could not meet their charting requirements because of difficulty getting physical access to the charts. This can be overcome by establishing a group therapy attendance binder for each group and modifying some of the documentation requirements.

Each group leader should have a three-ring binder for each of their groups. This binder should have a number of different parts: When you open the binder, the **Group Therapy Attendance Sheet** should be on top, followed by a series of tab dividers, one for each group member.

Behind each group member's tab divider should be: the problem list, the treatment plan for the target problem, and the **Session Documentation Form** for each group and individual therapy session. Having this documentation in the binder will make it readily available. These documents are copies of the originals that appear in the chart.

Group leaders can bring the attendance binder into group to document attendance. When group members are working on an issue, they can refer to the problem list and treatment plan. They can also quickly review the notes of past group and individual sessions.

Using the Group Therapy Attendance Sheet

The Group Therapy Attendance Sheet is used during the preparation session and the opening procedure. During the preparation session the group leader reviews each patient's participation history by looking at the coded entries on the attendance sheet. This gives the group leader the "big picture" of what has been happening with the group and with individual members.

The coding system consists of symbols that allow the leader to track various important elements of the group process. A check mark (✔) indicates the group member was present for the session. This is entered in the first of the two columns under each date. When the group member gives a reaction the group leader makes an "X" across the stem of the check mark (✔). This "Xed-off" check mark indicates the person gave a reaction.

When the group member volunteers to work, a dot is placed in the second column under that day (•). When the group member works in group, a circle is placed around the dot (⊙). If the person receives an assignment, the group leader adds an arrow to the circle (⊙ →) indicating the work was continued into the next session by giving an assignment. When the group member reports on the assignment in the next session, the group leader inserts a dot in the first column under that date next to the check mark (✔ •). With this coding system the group leader can tell at a glance who has been actively working in the group.

Progress Notes

To use this documentation system some traditional charting procedures need to be changed to incorporate the use of group and individual therapy progress notes. In traditional charting systems all documentation is entered into a running record in the chart. This means that all professionals involved in the treatment need physical access to the chart and write their notes in the correct time sequence in which they occurred. From a group therapy standpoint this creates problems. It means that group leaders must take notes

(Continued on page 61)

Group Therapy Attendance Sheet

Group: _____ Leader: _____

Day: _____ Time: _____ Coleader: _____

✔ = Present for Session	⊙ =	Worked on Issue
✔ = Had a Reaction	⊙ =	Had an Assignment
● = Volunteered to Work	✔● =	Reported on Assignment

Name	Dates of Groups														

CENAPS, 18650 Dixie Highway, Homewood, Illinois 60430 (phone: 708/799-5000) (© T. Gorski, 1985, 1992) during group sessions so they can remember what happened and then schedule time later to get the chart and write the chart entry from their notes. These notes are not available to them during group, because it is unrealistic to bring eight or ten charts into group sessions.

A more effective system can be designed by creating a standard progress note form for group and individual therapy sessions. This form should have three carbonized copies. The top (original) copy is placed in the patient's chart; the second copy is placed in the Group Therapy Attendance Binder; and the third copy is given to the group member to be kept in his or her personal recovery notebook.

Notes are still made in the running record, but they are brief and refer the reader to a section in the chart for group and individual session progress. A typical chart entry in the running record would be as follows:

4/12/94: Group Therapy: The patient attended group therapy. Refer to the group therapy progress note form for this date in the group and individual therapy note section of the chart. John Smith, Group Therapist.

The Session Documentation Form

The Session Documentation Form (see page 63) is a one-page form to be completed by the therapist and clients at the end of sessions. The client is asked to identify the **target problem** and complete four statements:

1. My target problem is...
2. The most important thing I learned in this session to help solve the target problem is...
3. What I am going to do differently as a result of what I learned is...
4. The assignment I am working to solve my target problem is...

There is a place for the group member's signature and date.

Part 2 of the form has five rating scales and a place for therapist notes. The rating scales are:

5. Stress Score
6. The Level of Functioning Outside of Sessions (GAF Score)
7. Problem-Solving Stage Score
8. Problem-Solving Motivational Response Score
9. Session Involvement Score
10. Client Satisfaction Rating

There is space for the therapist to enter a progress note, then sign and date the form.

The Psychosocial Stress Score (Item 5) and the GAF Score (Item 6) are completed during the opening procedure. All other scales and the progress notes are completed and reported during the closure exercise.

Standard Scoring Scales

The scores allow the therapist to evaluate the client quickly and efficiently in several areas. The exact scoring scales are presented later. It is important, however, to understand why scoring and scaling is important in the new environment of cost containment.

MCO case managers and other third-party payers want evidence that treatment works. They also want to see that patients are making progress as they move through the treatment process. You can show them this progress most easily by using standard scales and scoring systems. It doesn't mean much to say that a patient is getting better. It's far more valuable to say the patient's level of functioning improved by 30 percent as measured by changes in the GAF score from 30 to 60 and that the patient is progressing satisfactorily in problem solving by moving from a score of 0 on a problem-solving scale to 7 with a motivational response score increase from 3 to 8.

These scores may sound complicated, but they are easy to use and actually reduce the amount of time spent charting. Take a moment to study the Session Documentation Form. You will see that it can be used to document all types of sessions, including problem-solving groups. Then take the time to review the scoring for the standard scales. Using this form and carefully scoring each session will allow you to report quickly and efficiently on patient progress or problems.

Session Documentation Form

Client: _____ Therapist: _____

Type: ☐ Group ☐ Individual ☐ Psychoeducation ☐ Family ☐ Other _____

Day/Date/Time:_____

Part 1: Client Notes

1. My Target Probelem Is... _____

2. The most important thing I learned in this session to help solve the target problem is:

_____

_____

3. What I am going to do differently as a result of what I learned is...

_____

_____

4. The assignment I am working on to solve my target problem is:

_____

_____

Client Signature: _____ Date: _____

Part 2: Rating Scales and Notes

Person Completing the Rating:	Self	Leader
5. Stress Score:		
6. The Level of Functioning Outside of Sessions (GAF Score):		
7. Problem Solving—Stage Score:		
8. Problem Solving—Motivational Response Score:		
9. Session Involvement Score:		
10. Client Satisfaction Rating:		

Therapist's Progress Note: _____

_____

_____

_____

_____

_____

Therapist Signature:_____ Date: _____

The Problem-Solving Stage Scale

There are two problem-solving scores used. The first is the Stage Scale, which measures progressive movement in systematic problem solving. A score of 0 means no movement or not yet started in a problem-solving process. A score of 10 means the successful completion of the problem-solving process for the target problem. Here is the exact scale:

Problem-Solving Stage Scale

0 = Not rated
1 = No target problem identified
2 = Vague target problem identified
3 = Problem clarified
4 = The thoughts, feelings, and actions driving the target problem are identified and clarified
5 = List of alternative solutions developed
6 = Top three alternatives selected after analysis of benefits and disadvantages
7 = Consequences of top three alternatives projected
8 = Decision to use alternative is made
9 = Decision is implemented
10 = Outcome has been evaluated

Problem-Solving Motivational Response Scale

The Motivational Response Scale measures how actively the client is participating in the problem-solving process. Scores of 0-3 indicate active denial and resistance to systematic problem solving. Scores of 4-6 indicate varying levels of passive compliance with the standard process. Scores of 7-10 indicate self-motivated and proactive involvement in the problem-solving process.

Problem-Solving Motivational Response Scale

0 = Not rated
1 = Refuses to use systematic problem solving
2 = Severe denial and resistance
3 = Mild denial and resistance
4 = Passive resistance, appears to try while not fully applying self
5 = Compliance—does what is told, no more no less
6 = Active compliance—fully cooperates, no creative involvement
7 = Periodic creative involvement
8 = Consistent creative involvement
9 = Periodic self-directed problem solving
10 = Consistent self-directed problem solving

Session Involvement Scale

The Session Involvement Scale measures the client's ability to use the standard session format effectively. Scores of 1–3 are given to clients who do not fully comply with the basic rules and responsibilities of the session format. Scores of 4–7 are given to clients who adequately fulfill their rules and responsibilities but still need to develop proficiency at using the format to solve problems effectively. A score of 8–10 is given to people who have excellent skills at using the format to solve their problems.

Session Involvement Scale

0 = Did not rate
1–3 = Not complying with basic responsibilities and rules
4–7 = Average compliance with basic responsibilities and rules
8–10 = Excellent use of the format to solve problems

Stress Scale

The level of psychosocial stress that clients experience outside of the group session can have a lot to do with their level of performance in sessions. If performance during sessions drops, it is helpful to be aware of psychosocial stresses that can be causing difficulties in working during sessions. The Stress Scale, designed for use with DSM IV Axis 4, is helpful. A score of 0-3 is given to people with low levels of stress. A score of 4-7 is given to people with moderate levels of stress. A score of 7-10 is given to people who have severe stress.

Stress Scale

1. *Low Stress Level (Stress Score: 0–3)*
     - *Normal Stress of Day-to-Day Living*
     - *Stress Is Managed Well*
     - *No Subjective Distress or Dysfunction*
2. *Moderate Stress Levels (Stress Score: 4–6)*
     - *High Stress Levels*
     - *Stress Managed Poorly at Times*
     - *Stress Causes Subjective Distress but No Dysfunction*
3. *Severe Stress Levels (Stress Score: 7–10)*
     - *Very High Stress Levels*
     - *Stress Is Usually Managed Poorly*
     - *Stress Causes Subjective Distress and Dysfunction*

    Score 7 = Space Out
    Score 8 = Get Defensive
    Score 9 = Over React
    Score 10 = Can't Function

Client Satisfaction Scale

This scale rates the client's satsifaction with progress based on a ten-point scale with 0 being totally dissatisfied and 10 being totally satisfied.

Global Assessment of Functioning (GAF) Scale

The Global Assessment of Functioning (GAF) Scale is a rating of overall psychological, social, and occupational functioning used in completing a DSM IV Axis 5 evaluation. The GAF numerically scores the level of functioning between 001 (persistent suicidal and homicidal risk) to 100 (superior functioning).

This scale is such an important measurement of progress that I have decided to devote a separate section to its use. Many MCOs are using the GAF to determine the need for treatment. As a general rule patients with GAF scores above 70 are not approved for treatment. Scores of 30–60 qualify for outpatient treatment in various degrees of intensity. Patients with GAF scores of 30 and below qualify for residential or inpatient treatment for rapid stabilization.

The GAF score is also a useful way to describe progress systematically. Giving the initial GAF score and showing continuous improvements in GAF scores over the course of treatment is an easy yet effective way to measure progress and demonstrate that the treatment efforts are working.

Using the GAF Rating Scale

Step 1: Rate the severity of dysfunction caused by current problems or symptoms

Step 2: Rate the highest level of functioning in past year

Step 3: Set outcome goals using GAF scaling

Step 4: Report on progress using GAF scaling at the end of each session

---

Standard GAF Rating Procedure

There is a standard procedure for using the GAF rating scale. The first step is to rate the severity of dysfunction caused by the current problems or symptoms. The second step is to rate the highest level of functioning in the past year. This will show the previous level of functioning before the onset of the current problem.

The third step is to set outcome goals using GAF scaling. This means you identify the functional level using the rating scale that you would like the person to achieve by the completion of the current episode of treatment. The fourth and ongoing step is to report on progress using GAF scaling at the end of each session. This will show the effect that problem solving and treatment involvement have had on the overall functioning of the patient. Session-by-session evaluations using the GAF scale keep the focus where it belongs—on improving the ability to function effectively outside of sessions.

Determining Symptom Severity Using the GAF Scale

The first step of assigning a GAF score is to determine the client's general level of functional impairment. This is done by placing the client in one of three general categories of impairments in functioning: mild, moderate, or severe.

General Symptom Severity

1. *Normal Functioning (GAF Score: 71–100)*
   - *No Serious Symptoms*
   - *Normal Day-to-Day Stress*
   - *Feel Good and Functions Well*
2. *Mild Impairments in Functioning (GAF Score: 51–70)*
   - *Symptoms Are a Nuisance*
   - *But Can Always Be Managed With Extra Effort*
   - *Without Serious Social or Occupational Problems*
3. *Moderate Impairments in Functioning (GAF Score: 31–50)*
   - *Symptoms Periodically Cause Dysfunction in Spite of Extra Effort*
   - *Symptoms Cause Serious Social and Occupational Problems*
4. *Severe Impairments in Functioning (GAF Score: 1–30)*
   - *Symptoms consistently Cause Serious Dysfunction*
   - *Suicidal or Homicidal Risk*
   - *Inability to Function and Care for Self*

Normal functioning is rated between 71-100. There are no serious symptoms, normal day-to-day stress. In general the person feels good and functions well.

Mild impairments in functioning are rated between 51-70 and occur when symptoms or problems are a nuisance but can always be managed successfully with extra effort. There are no serious social or occupational problems, and aside from a feeling of personal or subjective stress, the client's life is going well.

Moderate impairments in functioning are rated with a GAF score between 31 and 50. The problems or symptoms periodically cause dysfunction despite extra efforts taken to manage them. There are also some serious social and occupational problems.

Severe impairments in functioning are rated with a GAF score between 1 and 30. The problems or symptoms consistently cause serious dysfunction. There is suicidal or homicidal risk and the inability to function and care for one's self.

The primary tool for determining general symptom severity is to ask the following diagnostic question: "When you are experiencing the problems or symptoms, how frequently are you able to manage them with extra effort and function normally?" If the answer is *almost always*, assign a mild GAF rating; if the answer is *sometimes*, assign a moderate GAF rating; and if the answer is *almost never* assign a severe GAF rating. The following table on pages 72–73 gives you guidelines for assigning precise GAF scores.

Global Assessment of Function Scale
Adapted from DSM IV by Terence T. Gorski

1. **Superior Functioning—GAF Score: 91–100 (Average Rating 95)**
   - *No Significant Symptoms or Problems*
   - *Superior Functioning in a Wide Range of Activities*
   - *Life Problems Never Seem to Get Out of Hand*
   - *Is Sought Out by Others Because of Many Positive Qualities*

2. **Above Average Functioning—GAF Score: 81–90 (Average Rating 85)**
   - *Absent or Minimal Symptoms*
   - *Good Functioning in All Areas*
   - *Interested and Involved in a Wide Range of Activities*
   - *Socially Effective*
   - *Generally Satisfied with Life*
   - *No More Than Everyday Problems or Concerns*

3. **Average Functioning—GAF Score: 71–80 (Average Score 75)**
   - *Transient Symptoms*
   - *Expectable Reactions to Psychosocial Stressers*
   - *No More Than Slight Impairment to Social, Occupational, or School Functioning*

4. **Mild Symptoms—GAF Score: 61–70 (Average Score 65)**
   - *Some Mild Symptoms or Some Diffuculty in Social, Occupational, or School Functioning*
   - *Generally Functioning Well*
   - *Has Some Meaningful Interpersonal Relationships*

5. **Moderate Symptoms—GAF Score: 51–60 (Average Score 55)**
   - *Moderate Symptoms that Create Periodic Dysfunction OR*
   - *Moderate Difficulty in Social, Occupational, or School Functioning*

6. **Periodic Severe Symptoms—GAF Score: 41–50 (Average Score 45)**
   - *Serious Symptoms that Create Periodic Dysfunction and Serious Subjective Distress*
   - *Serious Impairment in Social, Occupational, or School Functioning*

7. **Persistent Severe Symptoms—GAF Score: 31–40 (Average Score 35)**
   - *Some Impairment in Reality Testing and Communication OR*
   - *Major Impairment in Several Areas Such as Work or School, Family Relations, Judgment, Thinking, or Mood*

8. **Unable to Control Behavior—GAF Score: 21–30 (Average Score 25)**
   - *Behavior Influenced by Delusions, or Hallucinations OR*
   - *Serious Impairment to Communication or Judgment OR*
   - *Inability to Function in Almost All Areas*

9. **Periodic Danger to Self or Others—GAF Score: 11–20 (Average Score 15)**
   - *Some Danger to Self and Others OR*
   - *Occasionally Fails to Maintain Minimal Personal Hygiene*
   - *Periodically Unable to Care for Self*
   - *Gross Impairment in Communication*

10. **Persistent Danger to Self or Others—GAF Score: 1–10 (Average Score 5)**
    - *Persistent Danger of Harming Self or Others OR*
    - *Completely Unable to Care for Self*
    - *Suicidal Attempt with Clear Expectation of Death*
    - *Threat of Injury or Death to Others*

© Terence T. Gorski, CENAPS, 18650 Dixie Highway, Homewood, Illinois 60430 (phone: 708/799-5000)

CHAPTER 6

Group Responsibilities, Rules, and Corrective Discipline

It is important that each group member understand the basic rules and responsibilities of group members. These rules and responsibilities are not optional or flexible. Many group members tend to test limits and try to manipulate and avoid rules whenever possible. Therefore it is necessary to have strict rules and to enforce them consistently.

Group Responsibilities

The following is a statement of group responsibilities, rules, and standard format that are often explained to clients before entering the group. It is important to give them a written copy of these statements. Many programs ask members to sign a statement indicating they have reviewed and agree to comply with these responsibilities, rules, and format. This gives group leaders additional leverage should the member later refuse to comply. They can show the group member the signed agreement and ask what has changed.

71

As a group member you are responsible for:

1. Reactions to last session: It is your responsibility to give a reaction at the beginning of each group by telling the group three things: what you thought about the last session; how you felt about the last session; and the three group members who stood out to you and why they stood out. (See page 78 for more information.)

2. Completing and reporting on assignments: When you work on a problem or issue in group, the group leader may ask you to complete an assignment to help you make progress in solving that problem. It is your responsibility to complete all assignments in a timely fashion and report what you learned by completing it. (See page 79 for more information.)

3. Presenting problems to the group: You are expected to present a personal problem or issue to the group at least once every third group session. Recovery implies identifying and solving personal problems. It is expected that all group members are in group to learn how to solve problems that create pain and problems. (See page 80 for more information.)

4. Listening when others present problems: Group members are expected to pay attention and become actively involved when others are presenting problems. This is reflected in actively listening while other group member are discussing their problems, reporting what you heard them say, and asking them if you understood correctly.

5. Asking clarifying questions: Group members are expected to ask at least two or three intelligent and relevant questions to help clarify the problems that other group members present and help identify alternative solutions.

6. Giving feedback: Group members are expected to give feedback to other members who are working on problems. This feedback consists of telling the group members what you think their problem is and how you feel about him or her as a person.

7. Completing the closure exercise: Group members are required to complete a closure exercise at the end of each group by reporting the most important thing learned during that group session and what they intend to do differently as a result.

Group Rules

The basic rules for problem-solving group therapy are:

1. Punctuality and attendance: Group members are expected to attend all group sessions, arrive on time, and stay until the end of the session. Group members who miss more than one group session every six weeks may be asked to leave the group. Any group member arriving late for group will not be allowed to attend that session. Anyone who misses a group session without prior permission must make an appointment with the group leader to discuss the reason for his or her absence before being allowed to attend another group session.

2. Compliance with basic responsibilities: Membership in the group implies a willingness to comply with the seven basic group responsibilities described above.

3. Freedom of participation: Within the constraints of the standard format and basic responsibilities, you can say anything you want anytime you want to say it. Other group members have the right to give you feedback about what you say and how you say it. Silence is not a virtue in this group and can be antitherapeutic.

4. Right of refusal: With the exception of refusing to comply with basic group responsibilities, you can refuse to answer any questions or complete any assignments. Group members cannot force you to participate, but they do have the right to express how they feel about your silence or your choice not to get involved.

5. Confidentiality: What happens in the group stays among the members, with the exception of the group leaders who may consult with other members of the treatment team in order to provide more effective treatment and who may report any inappropriate behavior or violation of rules and responsibilities to the appropriate authority. Group members agree not to discuss with anyone else the content of the problems presented by other group members.

6. No violence: Acting out with physical or verbal violence within the group may be grounds for dismissal. Physical violence includes pushing, shoving, or hitting other group members. Verbal violence involves making threats, yelling, using profane language, or name calling. The threat of violence is as good as the act.

7. No dating, romantic involvement, or sexual involvement: Dating and romantic involvement or sexual involvement among group members is not allowed. Such activities can sabotage one or both persons' treatment. If such involvement starts to develop, it is to be brought to the attention of the group or your individual counselor at once.

8. Communication before termination: Anyone who decides to leave the group has a responsibility to inform the group in person before termination.

Corrective Discipline for Noncompliant Group Members

Correcting behavioral problems of group members is important, especially if the group has members who are involuntarily referred or who have a history of antisocial, disruptive, or acting-out behavior. As a general rule, breaches in the basic rules, responsibilities, and group agenda are viewed as therapy issues and dealt with in a therapeutic manner. This means that when these issues become a problem, the general treatment plan is temporarily abandoned and the group member's refusal or inability to comply with basic responsibilities becomes the target treatment problem until it is either corrected or the group member is transferred from the group.

There must be strict enforcement of group rules, responsibilities, and procedures. Group members often test limits, and if those limits are flexible they will test them repeatedly until the group leader establishes a firm limit. Therefore, group members must know that a systematic process will be used if they cannot or will not meet their basic responsibilities. These corrective discipline procedures should be reviewed with each person before entering the group.

The standard corrective discipline process usually involves a progression of three steps: the verbal warning, group problem-solving and feedback, and suspension or termination from the group. Let's look at each of these steps.

Step 1: The verbal warning: At the first violation the group leader points it out in group, then asks the group member if he or she recognizes the problem and is willing to correct it. If the group member agrees, no further action is taken. If the therapist suspects that the group member is not complying because of a personal problem or fundamental misunderstanding, an individual session may be scheduled to discuss the problem and develop an approach to solving it.

Step 2: Group problem-solving and feedback: If group members continue to violate the rules and responsibilities, the next step is to work on the self-defeating group behavior as a problem. Clients are asked to present their inability to follow the rules and responsibilities as they would any other problem. A standard problem-solving process is used, and this generally corrects the problem.

Step 3: Suspension or termination from group: If group members still cannot or will not comply with the basic rules and responsibilities, they cannot be allowed to continue in group. Their continued presence would inhibit the ongoing group process and prevent other group members from gaining maximum benefits of group involvement. This means that group members who cannot or will not comply must either be transferred to some other treatment modality or suspended from group until they are willing and able to comply with the rules.

It is important to note that none of this corrective process is done from a punitive point of view.

CHAPTER 7

The Standard Problem-Solving Group Agenda

An Overview

The standard eight-item agenda for problem-solving group therapy consists of: (1) Preparation, (2) Opening Procedure, (3) Reactions to Last Session, (4) Report On Assignments, (5) Setting the Agenda, (6) Problem-Solving Group Process, (7) Closure Exercise, and (8) Review and Evaluation. This chapter will provide a concise description of each part of this agenda. This will be followed by a detailed discussion of each component.

Preparation

The group leader prepares for group by reviewing a "thumbnail sketch" of each group member. This sketch includes each group member's demographic information, brief history, problem list, target problems, treatment plan (the sequential steps used to resolve the problem), and the current group assignment.

Group members prepare for group by reviewing their target problem, the sequence of problem-solving steps being used to resolve that problem, their current assignment, and their reactions from the last session.

Opening Procedure

The group leader enters the group room and takes a seat at the head of the group (if there is more than one group leader they seat themselves on opposite sides of the group). The leader asks the group members to arrange the chairs so everyone can easily see one another. New group members are briefly introduced. The group leader takes attendance and has a brief interaction with each group member. The group leader then leads a centering technique that helps group members to relax, notice their current thoughts and feelings, remember what happened in the last session, and remember which group members stood out to them and why.

Reactions to Last Session

The group leader asks the group members to give a two-minute reaction to the last session by completing five statements: (1) "I rate my level of stress since last session as...." (2) "I rate my level of functioning since last session as ...." (3) "What I thought about the last group session is...." (4) "How I felt about the last group session is...." and (5) "The three group members (other than the therapists) who stood out to me from last session are...and the reasons they stood out are...."

When giving a reaction, group members are asked to talk directly to the person they are reacting to, using the first person. An example would be: "John, you stood out to me because you were able to challenge the group leader. I would have been too afraid to do that and I respect you for it."

Report on Assignments

Each group member is asked to briefly answer the following questions about the group assignment they are currently working

---

Problem-Solving Group Therapy:
Standard Agenda

1. Preparation

2. Opening Procedure

3. Reactions to Last Session

4. Report on Assignments

5. Setting the Agenda

6. Problem-Solving Group Process

7. Closure Exercise

8. Review and Evaluation

---

on: (1) What is the target problem that you are trying to resolve? (2) What assignment are you currently working on? (3) What did you want to accomplishing by working on this assignment? (4) Did you complete the assignment? If yes, do you want time to work on the results in group? If no, why not and when will it be completed?

In problem-solving group therapy the primary goal is to identify and resolve target problems. By identifying their target problems at the start of each group, group members maintain the problem focus.

In order to resolve the target problem, group members need to set up an action plan consisting of a series of tasks. Each task is conceptualized as an assignment that is worked on in between group sessions and processed during the group. The group leaders keep the members focused on these tasks by asking them to identify their current assignment and the goal they want to accomplish by completing that assignment. This provides continuity in the problem-solving process and prevents problems from being forgotten or ignored.

This report on assignments is a brief report of not more than two minutes. If it is obvious the member needs to process a lot of information, or if he or she refused to do the assignment because of denial or resistance, the client's name should be entered on the agenda to work on the issues during the problem-solving portion of that group.

In group therapy you get what you "expect and inspect." It is the therapist's responsibility to give assignments (expect progress toward problem resolution), keep a record of all therapeutic assignments, and assure that these assignments are monitored (inspected) until the issue is resolved or the assignment is officially changed or discontinued by the therapist in group.

Setting the Agenda

After all assignments have been reviewed, the therapist sets the agenda by asking, "Who has an issue to work on in group?" Group members who have assignments to process or issues to work on indicate so at this time. The group leader will ask for a brief, thirty-second description of the problem and will ask if this is an emergency issue that must be dealt with immediately. The goal is to learn enough about the problem to be presented so it can be correctly prioritized when the agenda is set.

The therapist identifies all members who want to work and sets the order in which people will work. Group members who do not have time to complete their work in this group session will be first on the agenda in the following group session.

Problem-Solving Process

One person works at a time with the entire group involved in the problem-solving process. A standard problem-solving process is used that consists of five steps:

- **Problem presentation:** The problem presenter (the group member who is processing a problem in group) describes his or her problem to the group. The initial presentation of the problem is often vague, general, and incomplete. The member is asked, "Is there anything else we need to know to help you solve the problem?" several times. When the member either begins repeating or states he or she doesn't have anything else, the group begins to ask clarifying questions.

- **Questioning by the group:** The group begins to ask clarifying questions using an active listening model. Each group member asks a question, listens to the answer, tells the problem presenter what they heard, and confirms if they heard it correctly. The goal of group questioning is to clarify generalizations, deletions, and distortions in the original presentation of the problem. The focus is on the irrational thoughts, unmanageable feelings, and self-defeating behaviors that are related to the problem. The group leader acts as a teacher and coach in assisting other group members to target open-ended questions that clarify the core issues involved.

- **Feedback from group members:** The group members will each give feedback to the member who worked by answering two questions: (1) After listening to the problem presenter, what do you think the core problem is? (2) After listening to the problem presenter, how do you feel about him or her as a person?

- **Processing and assignment by the therapist:** The therapist summarizes the feedback and helps the problem presenter develop an assignment that will help him or her progress in the problem-solving process. The group leader may use specific therapy interventions at any point in the problem-solving process. It is recommended that these interventions be used infrequently to avoid making the group dependent on the leader to resolve all issues.

Most problems will not be solved by presenting them one time in group. One problem may require three to six presentations in group for full resolution to occur. Not every person will work on a problem during each session, but this doesn't mean that they are not benefiting from attendance. There is an 80/20 rule for group treatment. Approximately 80 percent of the benefit of group treatment occurs from learning how to become responsibly involved in helping others to solve their problems. Only 20 percent of the benefit is derived from working on personal problem issues.

Each group member has the responsibility to: (1) listen to other group members' problems; (2) ask questions to clarify the problem or proposed solution; and (3) give feedback about what they think the problem is and how they feel about the group member presenting the problem.

Closure Exercise

About fifteen minutes before the end of the group session, the leader stops the problem-solving process and passes out a **Session Documentation Form**, which asks group members to identify their target problem, the most important thing they learned that will help them to solve the target problem, what they are going to do differently as a result of what they learned, and the assignment they are working on. They are also asked to complete and report on five self-rating scales. Each group member briefly (two minutes or less) reports his or her answer to each question. The group leader writes a group note on the bottom of each worksheet for entry in the record. The time and place of the next group is confirmed and group is adjourned.

Review and Evaluation

After the group session, the group leaders meet to review the problems and progress of each group member, prevent therapy team burnout, and improve the group skills of the therapy team. A brief review of each group member is completed, outstanding group members and events are identified, progress and problems discussed, and the personal feelings and reactions of the therapy team reviewed.

The Group Agenda: Detailed Description

Now that you have a concise overview of how a problem-solving group therapy session is structured, each step of this group process will be reviewed in detail.

1. Preparation Session

The group leader prepares for group by reviewing a "thumbnail sketch" of each group member that includes a review of his or her demographic information and brief history, a review of the problem list and treatment plan, and a review of the issues the patient is most likely to work on in group.

Group members are expected to prepare for group by reviewing their target problem and the sequence of problem-solving steps they are following to resolve it, completing the current assignment they are working on, preparing their reactions from the last session, and practicing relaxation techniques that can help them to stay centered while working on problems in group.

2. Opening Procedure

The group leader establishes a therapeutic group climate by completing the following opening procedure. This procedure is conducted in the same way at the start of every group and becomes a ritual that helps everyone to get into a mind-set to work in group.

Enter the Room and Be Seated

The therapy team enters the group room and takes their seats. If there is a coleader, he or she should sit directly across from the therapist. This allows the leader and coleader to make eye contact with each other. It also divides the psychic energy of the group. If there are three staff members, they should seat themselves in the 12 o'clock, 4 o'clock, and 8 o'clock positions. The therapist checks to be sure that the chairs are arranged so that group members can easily see everyone else in the group.

The group leader then says something like this: "We are ready to start group. Please arrange your chairs in a tight circle. Make sure that you can easily see every other group member."

Take Attendance

The group leader takes attendance. During the attendance procedure, the group leader establishes intuitive contact by making eye contact and engaging in a brief conversation with each group member.

Attendance taking is a procedure that allows the therapist to assure that all group members are present and permits brief personal contact with each group member. It is recommended that a standard group attendance sheet be used (see page 60). As the therapist checks off each name on this list, a brief conversation is conducted with each group member.

The purpose of this conversation is for the therapist to establish personal contact with each group member and to develop a sense of where each group member is emotionally. A typical conversation between the therapist and group member during attendance-taking would be as follows:

Group Leader: John, how are you doing today?

John: Fine.

Group Leader: Could you put that in other words?

John: You know, I'm fine, okay. I feel relaxed and comfortable. I'm ready to get started.

Group Leader: Thank you, John. Good to see you. Nancy, how are you?

Nancy: I'm a little nervous. I did my assignment and I'm a little afraid to tell the group about it.

Group Leader: It's excellent that you did your assignment. It's also normal to be afraid before presenting it to the group. I'll be looking forward to hearing about that when we get to reports on assignments. Bill, how are you doing? (The process continues for all group members).

Introduce New Group Members

New group members are briefly introduced (two minutes or less) by welcoming them to the group, asking them to tell the group their name, briefly describe why they decided to join the group, and giving them permission to observe during the first group session.

A typical introduction by the therapist would be: "Today we have a new group member named Charlie. I'd like to welcome him to the group. Charlie, in two minutes or less would you tell us why you decided to join the group." The therapist listens and then says: "Charlie, during this session feel free to observe or to participate as actively as you wish. The only thing you need to do today is complete the closure exercise at the end of group. We'll expect you to get more active in the next group."

Conduct a Centering Exercise

The group leader conducts a centering exercise by asking everyone to take a deep breath, check what feelings and emotions they are bringing with them into the group, and do a brief body check. This is designed to get the group leader and group members in touch with themselves and leave nonrelated problems outside the group room so members can focus on their current thoughts and feelings. The group leader then asks everyone in the group to open their eyes and make eye contact with every other group member.

A centering technique should be used to help the members notice what they are thinking and how they are feeling. The goal is to set the stage for introspection. The following centering technique could be used:

"Let's take a moment to prepare for group. The time we are about to spend together is important. We have serious problems to work on with each other. Close your eyes. Take a deep breath, hold it for a moment, and exhale. Take another deep breath. Exhale. Notice what is happening in your body. Take another deep breath. Exhale. Notice the feelings and emotions that you are bringing with you into the group today. Take another deep breath. Exhale and notice the thoughts that are going on in your head. Now come back into the room and let's begin."

"Go back in your mind to the last group. Quickly review your memories of what happened. Notice any thoughts that you have about the last group. Notice any feelings you have about the last group. Recall three people who stood out to you in the last group and remind yourself why each one stood out.

"Open your eyes and make eye contact with every other group member."

When properly done this opening procedure warms up the group and gets them ready to work. Everyone has had an opportunity to have a brief interaction with the group leader, relax and get focused on the group, consciously review their thoughts and feelings from the last group, and make eye contact and get anchored into the group in the here and now. The stage is set for reactions to the last session.

3. Reactions to Last Session

The group leader asks group members to give a reaction to the last session. Every group member is expected to give a reaction from the last group. A reaction is given by each group member by completing these statements: "I rate my level of stress since last session as...." "I rate my level of functioning since last session as...." "What I thought about the last group session is...." "How I felt about the last group session is...." and "The three group members (other than the therapists) who stood out to me from last session are...and the reasons they stood out are...?"

Reactions to Last Session
1. I rate my level of stress since last session as....
2. I rate my level of functioning since last session as....
3. What I thought about last session is....
4. How I felt about last session is....
5. The three people who stood out and why are....

The reactions are not merely a report of what took place in the last session but a description of the feelings and thoughts that were generated in the members as a result of being in group. The reactions should indicate if the members were able to transfer what they learned during the last group into their daily lives.

A typical reaction made by a group member to the last group would be as follows:

- *What I thought about the last group session is...*

"What I thought about last group is that it was very productive. I learned a lot about how I deal with anger and frustration. There was a lot of good feedback when I talked about my problem."

- *What I felt about the last group session is...*

"What I felt about the last group session is a feeling of accomplishment as I worked on my problems. I was surprised. I got excited instead of depressed for the first time in a long time. I felt happy, proud, and pleased with myself!"

- *The three people who stood out to me and why are...*

"Joe, you stood out to me because you understood what I was talking about. Usually people look at me like I'm crazy when I start talking about what's really happening in my life, but you seemed to understand and accept me. I feel like we're coming from the same place.

"Mary, you stood out because you told me that you cared about me. I'm not sure if I believe you. A part of me thought you were telling the truth and I felt good. Another part of me said, 'Why should she care—no one else does.' I'm still not sure if you were being honest or just saying what you thought I wanted to hear.

"Pete, I was upset with you because you didn't seem to pay attention to me when I was talking. You just spaced out and acted like I wasn't there. A lot of people do this to me and I generally ignore it. But I'm supposed to try new things in group, so I decided to tell you and see what would happen."

Learning to Give Good Reactions

It takes time for the average group member to learn how to give good reactions in group. This learning takes place as a result of instruction and imitation. The group leader and other group members should explain the components of a good reaction to each new group member. A written handout should be provided that describes those components and gives examples. The group member also will learn by observing and imitating the reactions of other group members.

The following guidelines can help group members give good reactions:

1. When reporting your thoughts, start the sentence with the words, "I think ...".

2. When reporting your feelings, start the sentence with the words, "I feel..." or "I am experiencing ...".

3. Take time to breathe before and during your reactions so you can stay centered and stay in touch with your feelings. Pause briefly and take a deep breath. Notice the feelings in your throat, chest, and stomach. Breathe again and notice your thoughts (the self-talk or silent conversation going on in your head). Breathe again and notice any memories. Feel free to share any of these as they occur.

4. When giving feedback to others, look at them and make direct eye contact, and talk in the first person (in other words, use the word "you" instead of the words "he," "she," or "they").

The Goals of Giving Reactions

All group members are required to give a reaction to the last session. This accomplishes a variety of goals:

1. Communication training. Reactions provide training in basic communication skills and teach group members how to introspect, self-disclose, and give feedback.

2. Memory training. Reactions put pressure on group members to recall important events from previous group sessions. As a result, it serves as a memory training device. The person must connect what happened in the last group with what is going on in this group.

3. Continuity of group experience. Reactions force the therapist and group members to remember the significant events from the last group and to discuss them in this group. This provides a continuity of experience that allows progressive and sequential problem solving. It helps group members to become *time line competent* by linking past events to current experiences and projecting the logical consequences of their current behavior into the future.

4. *Development of social interest.* Reactions break the tendency toward isolation and self-centeredness by forcing group members to notice and comment on at least three other group members.

5. *Quickly sets therapeutic group climate.* Giving reactions quickly sets a therapeutic group climate by forcing each group member to both self-disclose and give feedback to other group members within the first ten to fifteen minutes of group.

6. *Tests the motivation of group members.* Reactions test the motivation of group members by asking them to comply with a simple procedure that demonstrates that they are involved and remember what is happening in group. Group members who refuse to give reactions generally have problems cooperating with other aspects of treatment. This should be a definite *red flag* that there are motivational problems with that group member.

7. *Therapist preparation.* Reactions provide an opportunity for the group leader to reflect on the last group and compare his or her personal memory with the group members' memories. The therapist can sit back while the group members complete a standard procedure and get centered on the group process. They can compare their memory to what other group members are saying, get centered, and ready themselves to perform at their best.

The Group Leader's Role in Reactions

The group leader's job is to facilitate the reaction. This is best done by using the following guidelines:

A reaction to last session is a one-way communication. One group member is not permitted to comment on the reactions made by another group member. If someone is upset by what another group member says, it is his or her responsibility to volunteer to work on the issue when the agenda is set.

A reaction is a no-fault communication.

There are no right or wrong reactions. The only feedback the therapist and other group members generally give is on the format and completeness of the reaction. In other words, the group members are reporting on their thoughts, feelings, and at least three persons who stood out to them from last session.

The group leader does not share his or her personal reactions to the last session. This is not done for several reasons. First, the group leader feedback will typically override the feedback from other group members because it is usually seen as more accurate and more powerful than the reactions of the other group members. Group members will often judge the "rightness" or "wrongness" of their own reactions based on what the therapist says. This can cause the group members to stop being honest and start trying to imitate the therapist.

If the group leader gives personal reactions, he or she loses a sense of objectivity and may run the risk of becoming locked into the dynamics of the group instead of facilitating it. Should their feedback hook an adverse reaction in a group member, the therapist would be in a poor position to facilitate objective problem resolution.

4. Report on Assignments

Assignments are an important part of problem-solving group therapy. The goal is to identify problems that group members wish to resolve and then set up an action plan for their resolution. Continuity in the problem-solving process is created by the use of assignments that allow members to work on their problems between group sessions and then report on their progress.

There are two primary purposes for having group members report on their assignments in each group: accountability and continuity. The **rule of accountability** states, *"You only get what you expect and inspect."* If you expect a client to complete an assignment, you should be willing to inspect the outcome by monitoring the group member's progress and evaluating whether the assignment produces the outcome that was expected.

The **law of continuity** states, *"An assignment will only be completed if the group member knows that his or her progress will be systematically monitored in each group."* This monitoring assures that all assignments are either completed or evaluated and changed. The monitoring process assures that assignments are not forgotten, allowing the patient to defocus from the process of solving the target problem.

A group member completes a report on an assignment by answering the following questions:

- *"What assignment did you have and what did you hope to learn by completing it?"* This question assures that the group member remembers what the assignment was and understands the goal in completing the assignment.

- *"Did you complete the assignment?"* This question holds group members directly responsible for completing the assignment. If group members completed the assignment they are asked, *"What did you learn from completing the assignment?"* This is a brief report that shouldn't take longer than a minute to complete. I often ask the member to answer this question in twenty-five words or less. If it is obvious that the member needs to process a lot of information, the exploration of the assignment should be entered on the agenda for later work during the problem-solving portion of that group.

Report on Assignments

1. What was your assignment?
2. Did you do it?
3. What did you learn from it?

If group members fail to complete the assignment they are asked, *"Why didn't you complete the assignment?"* If resistance appears to be part of the failure to complete the assignment and the group leader feels a need to process the resistance in depth, the discussion should be entered on the agenda for later work during the problem-solving portion of that group.

As a general rule group leaders only get what they "expect and inspect." It is the group leader's responsibility to expect group members to meet their responsibilities. The group leader does this by giving assignments (expecting progress toward problem resolution), keeping records of all therapeutic assignments, and assuring that these assignments are monitored (inspected) until the issue is resolved or the assignment is officially changed or discontinued by the group leader in group.

Group members are responsible for completing all assignments they agree to complete. Problem solving in group is a collaborative process and group members have the right to negotiate what assignments they take on. Once they agree to complete an assignment, however, they are held responsible for meeting that commitment unless the group leader and the group members (clients) agree that it is not useful to pursue the issue further.

5. Setting the Agenda

The goal of setting the agenda is to assure that group members who have an issue to work on in group can identify themselves and group members can be selected to work based on the seriousness of their problem and how frequently they have worked in past sessions.

Who has an issue to work on in group?

The group leader sets the agenda by asking, "Who has an issue to work on in group?" An issue can be either a new problem the group member wants to bring up, the completion of an assignment from a previous group, or the completion of an exercise from some standard workbook such as *The Staying Sober Workbook.**

The Staying Sober Workbook by Terence T. Gorski provides a detailed series of exercises for relapse prevention. This workbook is an ideal companion to problem-solving group therapy. It is available from Herald House/Independence Press.

Setting the Agenda
1. Who has an issue to work on?
2. What is the issue?
3. Is it an emergency?

Briefly Describe the Problem

The group leader asks for a brief, one-minute description of the problem and if this is an emergency issue that must be dealt with immediately. The problem presenters (group members who have a problem they want to work on in group) may say something like this:

I nearly got drunk last week after an argument with my husband. He got jealous when we were at a party and stormed out without me after publicly accusing me of flirting with another guy at the party. I was embarrassed and nearly went to the bar and started drinking. Fortunately a friend was there who asked me if I wanted a ride home and we left together. I'm still upset about it and have been thinking about drinking ever since. I'm afraid I might relapse and I don't know what to do.

It is important to remember that you are setting the agenda and not trying to solve the problem. The correct response of the therapist is to simply say, "Thank you, who else would like to get on the agenda to work tonight?"

If the therapist immediately begins trying to solve the problem, the standard agenda will be violated. The goal is to learn enough about the issue that the group member wants to present so it can be correctly prioritized when the agenda is set.

The group leader will identify all the members who want to work (we will call these group members "problem presenters") and establish the order in which people will work. Group members who do not have time to complete their work in this group session will be first on the agenda in the following group session. Care needs to be taken not to begin the problem-solving process until all people with issues to work on have been identified.

When people volunteer to work at the beginning of a group they are committed and generally do not back out later. If, however, the group leader starts working with the first person who volunteers, other group members may become reluctant to work as the group sessions continues.

The Importance of Timing and Pacing

It is important to keep the opening procedures, reactions to last session, report on assignments, and setting the agenda strictly time limited. The group leader can do this by setting the time frame for each exercise. For example: "We have about fifteen minutes to complete assignments. This means each of you will get about two minutes each. Who would like to begin?" or "It's time for group members to report briefly on the assignments you have been working on. Remember, this is a brief update that should take only one to two minutes. If you need more time to discuss your assignment, raise your hand when I set the agenda and I'll be happy to schedule time later in the group."

During these first procedures cross talk in the group should be kept to a minimum. The therapist should have a no-nonsense, "taking care of business" attitude. This attitude should be warm and friendly but communicate that there is a job to get done so everyone can get on to the most important part of the group—the problem-solving segment.

Many group leaders, in an effort to save time, skip one or more of these procedures. Most find that in the long run they accomplish less. Group therapy research shows very clearly that effective therapy groups must complete three phases: warm-up, climax, and closure. During the warm-up period group members get centered and break the ice to become involved in the group process. During the climax the group is involved in working on serious and often intense issues. During the closure group members have an opportunity to review in their minds what happened in group, share what they learned, and how they are reacting emotionally to the group.

If there is not a sufficient warm-up, the group does not get into working on serious or intense issues. This is because people are not feeling safe and comfortable. In problem-solving group therapy, this warm-up period is provided by the opening procedure, reactions to last session, report on assignments, and setting the agenda.

It is the therapist's job to use appropriate timing and pacing. If you hurry through these exercises too quickly and superficially, the group never gets warmed up and it dead-ends during problem solving. If, on the other hand, the group therapist spends too much time on warm-ups, the group members get bored and turned off, and valuable time that could have been spent on problem solving is lost. It is up to the therapist to find an appropriate balance between these two extremes.

6. The Problem-Solving Process

Once the group is warmed up, it is time to begin working on the individual problems of the problem presenters. One problem presenter works at a time, with the entire group involved in the problem-solving process. Typically each problem presenter will work for about thirty minutes. During group problem solving, all members have the responsibility to listen to other group members' problems, ask relevant clarifying questions, and give feedback about what they think the problem is and how they feel about the person. Self-disclosure must be managed carefully to keep the primary focus on the patient who is working on the issue. The standard problem-solving process consists of five steps: problem presentation, group questioning, therapeutic processing by the group leader, group feedback, and summary and assignment. Let's look at each of these steps in more detail.

Problem-Solving Group Process

A. Problem Presentation
B. Group Questioning
C. Therapeutic Processing by the Group Leader
D. Group Feedback
E. Summary and Assignment

A. Problem Presentation

The problem presenter explains his or her problem or assignment to the group. This initial presentation of the problem is often vague, general, and incomplete. The member is asked several times, "Is there anything else we need to know to help you solve the problem?" When the member either begins repeating or states he or she doesn't have anything else, the group begins to ask clarifying questions.

B. Group Questioning

The group asks clarifying questions using an active listening model. The questioner (the group member who is asking the question) uses a standard formula for asking questions: ask a question, listen to the answer, tell the problem presenter what was heard, confirm if it was heard correctly.

The first step is to *ask a question* that is useful in solving the problem. Useful questions are clear, relevant, and intelligent. A clear question is easy to understand. A relevant question is directly related to the problem. An intelligent question gives the person answering it a new way of thinking or looking at a problem.

The second step is to *listen to the answer.* Many people ask a question and then begin to think about the next question before they hear or respond to the answer. They shoot off a string of questions, leaving the problem presenter feeling interrogated rather than understood. This is avoided by listening carefully to each answer.

> ## Standard Formula for Asking Questions
> 1. Ask a question.
> 2. Listen to the answer.
> 3. Tell the problem presenter what was heard.
> 4. Confirm if it was heard correctly.

The third step is to *tell the problem presenter what you heard*. This is done by paraphrasing. Paraphrasing involves repeating what you heard the problem presenter say. Good paraphrasing begins with the words, "What I am hearing you say is...". Here is an example: "What I am hearing you say is that your husband is very jealous and you are getting tired of the way he tries to control you?" Paraphrasing the answer helps the problem presenter to feel listened to, understood, taken seriously, and affirmed as a person.

The fourth step is to *confirm if you heard it correctly*. Ask the problem presenter, "Did I understand you correctly" or "Did I get it right"? By asking for confirmation, an intense dialogue between the questioner and the problem presenter usually emerges. This dialogue is the heart of the problem-solving process.

It is important to remember that most problem presenters don't have a clear understanding of what their problem is. They know they are in pain and that something is wrong. They have a general idea of what is wrong but usually have not thought the problem through.

Group questioning helps problem presenters think about their problems in a systematic way in order to gain perspective and insight. Problem presenters gain perspective as group members ask how this problem relates to other areas of their lives. They gain insight as they begin to see new cause-and-effect relationships they couldn't see before.

Using open-ended and closed questions. The use of open-ended questions is strongly encouraged for drawing out information. An open-ended question is one that *cannot* be answered by a yes or no answer. A closed question is one that *must* be answered by a yes or no answer. Closed questions give very little information. Open-ended questions give much more information. The question, "Are you married?" is a closed question that will tell very little. This can be turned into an opened-ended question by asking, "Tell me what your current love relationship is like." This will give far more information.

Closed questions are recommended for getting a commitment to confirm or deny specific information. For example, after the group member describes his or her relationship, you might ask the question, "Are you saying that alcohol and drugs have caused problems in your marriage?" This use of closed questions forces the problem presenter to make a commitment to a definite and specific answer.

Keeping the problem focus. It is important to keep the focus on the issue of solving the targeted problem and the related irrational thoughts, unmanageable feelings, and self-defeating behavior. To do this the group members need to learn how to ask problem-focused questions. When dealing with people who have behavioral health problems, several problem-focused questions can be used.

The term **target problem** refers to the primary problem or disorder being treated. This could be chemical dependency, depression, anxiety, antisocial behavior, or other primary disorders. The term **target behavior** refers to the primary, self- defeating behaviors that are related to the target disorder. In the case of chemical dependency, for example, the use of alcohol and drugs would be the target behavior. In the case of antisocial personality, the use of manipulative or criminal behaviors would be the target behaviors.

- When was the last time you used the target behavior?
- When was the last time you had an urge or desire to use the target behavior?
- What problems or situations created the urge to start using the target behavior?

- How does the problem you are currently working on relate to your use of the target behavior?
- How does the problem you are currently working on affect your ability to recognize that you have a serious problem with the target behavior and need to make it a priority to stop using the target behavior?
- How did this problem affect your willingness or ability to stay abstinent from the target behavior and maintain your recovery program?
- How did this problem set you up to start using the target behavior in the future?

Transitioning between thoughts, feelings, and actions. Another strategy for questioning involves helping the problem presenter clarify the thoughts, feelings, and behaviors related to the target problem. This can be accomplished by asking the problem presenter to describe the problem, and then asking him or her to identify and clarify the thoughts, feelings, and actions that are related to the problem. Here is an example of how this is done.

Questioner: Could you tell me about the problem you want to work on?

Problem Presenter: The problem is that every time I get a paycheck I feel the urge to start using cocaine.

Questioner: Can you remember the last time this happened?

Problem Presenter: Yes, it happened last Friday when I got paid. I picked up the paycheck, and as I started walking out of the building I started thinking about how good it would feel to get some cocaine.

Questioner: Can you remember exactly what you started to think?

Problem Presenter: Yes. I started thinking that I had a lot of cash. I worked hard for it and I deserved some good times. I had enough money to spend a little of it on cocaine. It would help me relax and make me feel better.

Questioner: What I'm hearing you say is that when you have money in your pocket you start to think that you worked hard and deserve to have a good time. You also start to think that cocaine

99

will make you feel better, you can afford it, and you can get away with it, so why not? Is that right?

Problem Presenter: Yes, you've got it.

Questioner: When you are thinking that way, what are you feeling?

Problem Presenter: I'm not sure.

Questioner: Think about it for a moment. Which of these words sounds closest to what you are feeling? Are you mad? ...sad? ...glad? ...or scared? Which one of those words sounds closest to what you feel?

Problem Presenter: I guess the word "mad." I feel angry because I can't use cocaine. It's the only thing that I know how to do to relax and have a good time. It's the only way I can turn off the stress.

Questioner: So you feel angry because if you can't use cocaine, you don't have any other way to turn off the stress, relax, and have a good time. Is that correct?

Problem Presenter: Yes.

Questioner: When you are feeling that way, what do you have an urge to do to deal with that feeling?

Problem Presenter: I want to use cocaine!

Questioner: What do you want the cocaine to do?

Problem Presenter: I want it to relax me, make me feel good, let me have a good time.

Questioner: So you have an urge to relax, feel good, and have a good time but you don't know any other way to do it.

Problem Presenter: That's right.

Questioner: What do you actually do?

Problem Presenter: I go home alone determined not to use and sweat it out.

Questioner: Is there any way besides using cocaine that you could relax, feel good, and have a good time?

Notice the sequence of questions: Tell me about the problem. When you experience that problem, what do you tend to think? When you are thinking that way, what do you tend to feel? When you are feeling that way, what do have an urge to do? When you feel the urge to do that, what do you actually do? Can you think o another way to cope with the problem? This sequence of questioning transitions from the problem to the related thoughts, feelings, action urges, and actual behaviors.

Challenging generalizations, deletions, and distortions. Group questioning also can be used to clarify generalizations, deletions, and distortions in the original presentation of the problem. A **generalization** is a statement that is all-inclusive, such as "Everything is going wrong!" This is challenged by asking the clarifying question "What do you mean 'everything is going wrong'? Can you be more specific and give us an example of exactly what is going wrong?"

A **deletion** is a statement that fails to give necessary information. A group member may say, for example, "I got angry." This is an incomplete statement because it fails to explain who or what he got angry at, what happened that caused him to become angry, and how he acted out his anger. This is challenged by asking the clarifying questions: "Who did you get angry with? What did he or she do that caused you to get angry? What did you do after you got angry?"

A **distortion** is a statement that blows something out of proportion or distorts the real facts. Distortions often involve figures of speech that are not helpful in solving a problem. Group members may say, "He blew me away!" This is a distortion because in reality the person was not blown away. It would be more helpful to ask the clarifying question, "What exactly did the person do that blew you away?" Another way to clarify this distortion would be to ask, "What exactly happens to you when you get blown away?" Another example would be a group member who says, "He treated me like crap?" Again the question, "What exactly did he do to treat you like crap?" can help clarify.

The role of the group leader in group questioning. It is important to understand the role of the group leader in group questioning. The group leader usually *should not* ask the problem presenter questions directly. If the group leader starts asking the questions, the group process quickly degenerates into an individual therapy session with an audience.

The group leader *should* get the other group members to ask the questions that need to be asked. This is done in one of four ways: (1) by making commercial announcements, (2) by coaching and directing individual group members who are asking questions, (3) by calling time outs to discuss group dynamics that are emerging during the questioning process, and (4) demonstrating the questioning process. Let's explore each of these ways of getting group members to ask targeted and strategic problem-solving questions.

Making commercial announcements. A commercial announcement is a thirty-second "mini-lecture" that gives the entire group information about how to improve the questioning process. No single group member is singled out. Typically, group leaders establish a time-out signal that lets the group know they want to make a commercial announcement. I usually give the time-out signal used by a football coach and say something like this: "Excuse me, it's time for a commercial announcement." I then give the information or suggestions that are appropriate and say, "End of commercial." The group usually hears the information and adjusts their questioning style accordingly. Here are some of the typical commercial announcements that are used most frequently:

- **Commercial announcement #1: Closed vs. Open Questions.** "When asking questions you can get more information by asking an open-ended question that cannot be answered with a 'yes' or 'no' answer. Instead of asking, 'Do you have a job?' which is a closed question, ask, 'Will you tell us about your current job?' which is an open-ended question. End of commercial."

- **Commercial announcement #2: Lack of Eye Contact.** "It's important to look at the person and use his or her first name when you are asking questions. This allows you to connect with the person and make him or her feel listened to and visible. If the person you are questioning isn't looking at you, it is OK to say something like 'Could you look at me for a moment?' End of commercial."

- **Commercial announcement #3: Defocusing from the Target Problem.** "It is very important to keep the questions focused on the problem presenter's target problem. One way problem presenters set themselves up to avoid dealing with their target problem is to invite the group to follow an interesting but irrelevant tangent. If you are not sure what the target problem is, you are probably off track. You can get back on track by asking, 'We seem to be getting off track, will you tell me again what the target problem is that we are working on?' End of commercial."

- **Commercial announcement #4: Giving Advice.** "The goal right now is to ask questions, not to give advice. You want to find out information and clarify it, not tell or suggest things for the person to do. If you give advice most people get defensive and don't take it anyway. You can always convert a statement of advice into a question or a series of questions. For example, if you want to say 'You should go to more Twelve Step meetings!' (advice), you can ask instead, 'How many Twelve Step meetings do you attend each week? How do your meetings help you in working on this issue? What benefits and disadvantages do you see in attending more meetings? What could you do differently at your meetings to help you deal with this problem?' These questions will lead problem presenters to the conclusions you want them to have. Because they figured it out for themselves as a response to your questions, they are more able to accept it, take ownership of it, and put it to work in their lives. End of commercial."

- **Commercial announcement #5: Self-disclosing Instead of Questioning.** "At times the group members will stop asking questions and start self-disclosing. An example of this would be: 'I want to ask you about how many AA meetings you attend because I know that they helped me. When I first started attending meetings I ...'. This is generally not helpful during the questioning period. By telling the problem presenter about yourself and your reactions instead of focusing on clarifying questions that can help him or her to solve the target problem, you can defocus the entire problem-solving process. End of commercial."

Coaching and directing group members who are asking questions: Another method to get the answers you need without directly questioning the problem presenter is to coach the group member who is asking the questions. Many group members will go in the right direction by asking clarifying questions, but the problem presenter gets anxious or uncomfortable with the focus of the questioning and he or she just stops. Here you can begin working with the questioner by saying things like this: "Don't stop now! You're going in the right direction. If you're afraid that you are getting too pushy or might hurt John's feelings, ask him if he wants you to stop or if you should keep going!"

You can also show the questioner how to sequence a series of questions that gets the needed information. You could say something like this: "You were on the right track a few minutes ago. Why don't you try asking about how this problem is affecting John's family?"

Time outs to discuss the group questioning process. At times the group gets stuck in the questioning process and no one in the group can seem to get on track. This often happens with problem presenters who are extremely guarded or defensive. The group leader can call a time out by saying something like this: "Let's take a time out to discuss what is going on. Do you think we are making any progress? What do you think is hanging us up? What is John doing that's blocking you from getting the answers you need? How are you allowing John to get you off track? Do you see the traps that John is throwing in front of you to throw you off track?"

Invite the problem presenter to listen and become involved. Remember, the goal is for the group members to learn new problem-solving skills. This usually happens when you create a comfortable environment for people to look at themselves and their problem-solving skills.

Demonstrating the questioning process. At times it is appropriate for the group leader or coleader to demonstrate the questioning process by directly asking the problem presenter questions. As we discussed earlier, as a general rule this is not a good idea because the group members tend to stop asking questions, detach, and allow the group leader to do all the work.

Sometimes, however, a problem presenter will be presenting a particularly difficult problem that the group members don't have the skills to deal with. In such cases a few carefully selected focusing questions can accelerate the problem-solving process and get the problem presenter through an impasse or stuck point. This can be important role modeling, but it should be done infrequently.

Spectator therapy and the problem-solving process. Not every person will work on a problem during each session, but this doesn't mean that they are not benefiting from attendance. There is an 80/20 rule for group treatment: 80 percent of the benefit of group treatment occurs from learning how to become responsibly involved in helping others solve their problems. In other words, most group members get more benefit from listening to the problems of other group members, asking questions, and giving feedback than they do out of working on their own issues. Only 20 percent of the benefit is derived from working on personal problem issues.

C. *Therapeutic Processing by the Group Leader*

The group leader may use a specific therapy technique to assist the patient in the problem-solving process. The most commonly used techniques involve guided imagery for mental rehearsal and role playing for skill training. Care should be taken not to make the group dependent on the leader to resolve all issues. It is recommended that the leader use individual techniques not more often than every two to three patients who work in group. At times, the therapeutic processing may occur after feedback from the group members.

D. *Group Feedback*

After about fifteen or twenty minutes of group questioning, the group leader stops the process and instructs the group members to give feedback to the problem presenter by answering two questions: (1) What is your understanding of the problem that this person is working on? and (2) After listening to the person work on the problem, how do you feel about him or her as a person? The group leader will often ask group members to give feedback by completing two statements: (1) "I think your problem is...", and (2) "My feelings about you as a person are...".

As group members get better at giving feedback the leader can also ask them to tell the problem presenter the strengths they see that will help him or her solve the problems and the weaknesses they see that may get in the way of solving the problem. This can be done by asking the group member giving the feedback to complete two statements: (1) "The strengths I see that will help you solve the problem are..." and (2) "The weaknesses I see that will interfere with your solving the problem are...".

Each group member should be allowed no more than two or three minutes to give feedback. Group members need to learn how to get to the point, say what they mean, and then move on. Most group members will tend to get sidetracked and give lengthy feedback that misses the point. It is helpful for the group leader to assist group members in giving feedback that clearly and concisely presents their main point or message.

It is important to remember that there is a limited amount of group time. If each member in an eight-person group spends two minutes giving feedback, that will take sixteen minutes or half of the allotted time to work on a problem. It is also important to remember that the person receiving the feedback has limits to what he or she can integrate and remember. Feedback that is short, clear, and concise is more likely to be remembered.

E. Summary and Assignment by the Group leader

At the end of the feedback, the group leader summarizes the main points of feedback given by the group. The group leader will often begin his or her summary by saying, "Let me summarize what I am hearing the group tell you." The leader should limit the summary to the three most important points the problem presenter needs to hear. The group leader will then help the problem presenter develop an assignment that will help him or her to progress in the problem-solving process. The process of giving assignments will be

106

described in more detail later when we review the problem-solving process.

7. The Closure Exercise

At the end of group it is important for each group member to have time to sort out their thoughts and feelings and make sense out of what happened in the group. To do this the group leader uses a **Session Documentation Form** (see page 63), which asks group members to identify the most important thing they learned in group and what they are going to do differently as a result of what they learned.

In some groups the closure exercise is done verbally by having each group member answer the questions in group. In other groups the group members combine the closure exercise with a self-report form that greatly simplifies documentation and integrates it into the group process.

About fifteen minutes before the scheduled end of the group, the group leader passes out the Session Documentation Form. The top half of the form asks group members to identify their target problem, describe the most important thing they learned in the session to help them solve the target problem, what they are going to do differently as a result of what they learned, and the assignment they are working on to solve their target problem. The bottom half of the form contains a place for the group leader to make group therapy notes. The documentation form contains three copies. The top copy goes into the chart or clinical record; the middle copy is kept by the group therapist in the client's therapy notebook; the bottom is kept by the group member as a personal record of what is happening in the group sessions.

The group leader passes out the form and all group members complete it. This takes about two minutes. Each group member tears off the bottom copy and turns in the top two copies to the group leader. Group members take two or three minutes to review their answers. While they are answering, the group leader writes down a brief note about the group members' participation in group, tells each group member what he or she has written, and then moves on to the next group member.

The Closure Exercise

1. My target problem is ....
2. The most important thing I learned in group to help me solve my target problem is....
3. What I am going to do differently as a result of what I learned is....
4. The assignment I am working on to solve my target problem is....

Using this method many group therapists find they can complete most or all of their documentation before the end of group. The closure forms then become the basic documents used in the review and evaluation session where the group notes are finalized.

8. Review and Evaluation

The review and evaluation session is critical for both the group leaders and the members. The group leaders usually review and evaluate the group session immediately after it is over. This is often called a debriefing session and is designed to review the group members' problems and progress, prevent therapy team burnout, and improve the group skills of the therapy team. During the review and evaluation session a brief review of each patient is completed, outstanding group members and events are identified, progress and problems are discussed, and the personal feelings and reactions of the therapy team are reviewed.

Group members are encouraged to review and evaluate the group session with other group members. This usually takes the form of encouraging group members to have coffee together after the group and discuss their reactions. The "coffee klatch" is often more therapeutic than the group session itself.

Group members are also encouraged to think back on the group each day and use what they learned in their day-to-day life. They are encouraged to keep a journal of their group experiences to remember what they learned and how they applied that new learning to solving their problems.

The Review Session Format

The following format can be used as a guideline for doing group debriefing:

Part 1: Group Member Review. Start the debriefing session by briefly reviewing the progress and problems of each group member. As you do this check the group closure exercise form and make sure the group notes section is complete and accurate.

Part 2: Outstanding Group Members. Describe the group members who stood out the most in today's group and why they stood out. Group members usually stand out because they did an exceptionally good job, a noticeably poor job, or somehow hooked the group leaders either positively or negatively. These strong reactions need to be explored. Feeling really good about a group member can block objectivity and lead to enabling or preferential treatment. Feeling bad about a group member can set up unnecessary conflict that distracts from the execution of the treatment plan.

Part 3: Outstanding Events. Discuss any outstanding positive or negative events in the group. Again, the goal is to identify what these outstanding events are hooking in the group leader.

Part 4: Group Problems and Progress. Discuss any problems or progress observed in the overall management of the group. This is the time to look at the dynamics and maturity of the group as a whole. A group is more than just a collection of individual members. There is a synergism that occurs as the group members work together. Each group has its own personality and temperament, as well as its own unique strengths, weaknesses, and problems. It is important to keep track of how the group as a whole is maturing, developing, and changing.

Part 5: Personal Feelings and Reactions. Discuss any personal feelings and reactions about the group, group members, or therapy team members. This is the time to get honest about any strong feelings or reactions. Group therapy is a powerful process that often hooks personal feelings and issues in the group leaders. If these reactions are recognized and dealt with early, the process of running a group can be a proactive personal growth experience for the leaders as well as the members. If these issues are not dealt with, the group leaders take these feelings and issues home with them as they often lose their objectivity and begin doing things in group that harm the group process.

CHAPTER 8

The Standard Problem-Solving Process

A problem is rarely solved in one group presentation. To solve a single problem often requires three to six group presentations. As a result, each problem needs to be broken down into chunks that can be worked on in twenty- to thirty-minute segments. In order to break the problem down we need to understand the standard problem-solving process. This standard process should be used in both group and individual therapy and consists of three general steps: (1) problem identification and clarification; (2) identification of alternatives and consequences; and (3) decision, action, and evaluation.

Step 1: Problem Identification and Clarification

The first step in problem-solving is problem identification and clarification. When group problem presenters identify a problem they answer the question, "What is the problem and how is it affecting you?" At this stage the problem is usually vague and general because the problem presenter knows that something is wrong but can't clearly explain what is wrong. The process of clearly explaining what the problem is leads naturally into problem clarification.

The Standard Problem-Solving Process
1. Problem identification and clarification
2. Identification of alternatives and consequences
3. Decision, action, and evaluation.

The group begins clarifying the problem by asking, "Is there anything else that we need to know to help you solve the problem?" They then ask questions about the details of the problem and how the problem relates to the problem presenter's target problem. Typical clarifying questions involve who, what, when, where, why, and how questions.

- *Who* is involved in this problem?
- *What* are you or other people doing that is causing or complicating the problem?
- *When* did this problem first start?
- *Why* are you interested in solving the problem right now? (Why didn't you solve it yesterday or put it off until tomorrow?)
- *How* is this problem affecting you or other people?

A good clarifying strategy is to ask the problem presenter to tell a story about how this problem occurred in the past and how it is likely to occur in the future. By listening carefully to the stories, the leaders and group members can often hear aspects of the problem that would remain hidden otherwise. The current problem can also be related to other things in the group member's life by asking, "What other problems are there in your life that are similar to or related to this problem?"

Remember to keep the focus on the target problem by asking about how the problem can create an urge to relapse, discourage the problem presenter from practicing his or her recovery program, or activate the target problem or disorder.

Problem identification and clarification usually takes two group sessions. In the first session the group member presents the problem and responds to questions. The answers given by the problem presenter typically show that he or she is confused about the problem and really isn't sure about what is going on. This general confusion is presented to the client in the feedback from other group members.

The group leader then gives the problem presenter an assignment to clarify the problem. This often involves writing a problem statement or interviewing other group members who have had similar problems. In the second group the problem presenter brings up the problem again, and this time he or she can usually clarify the problem sufficiently to start looking at alternative solutions.

Step 2: Identifying Alternatives and Consequences

The second step of problem solving involves identifying alternatives and consequences. The problem presenter is told there is always more than one way to solve a problem. Good problem presenters usually can identify at least three different ways of solving the problem that have a good chance of working. These different ways of solving a problem are called alternatives.

Alternative solutions are identified by asking group members to find out what the problem presenter has done in the past to try and solve this problem and which of those past efforts were helpful and which were not helpful. Group members can also explain what they have done in the past when they have had a similar problem or what they know that other people have tried. The problem presenter and other group members are then asked what new ideas they can come up with that could help solve this problem. The problem presenter should write a list of the alternative solutions identified during the group.

Each alternative solution will produce different consequences if the problem presenter attempts to use it. Although you cannot predict precisely what will happen, logical thinking will determine possible benefits and disadvantages of each alternative. This can then become an assignment: take each alternative solution and identify the best, worst, and most likely things that could happen if you tried to solve the problem this way.

Typically the process of identifying alternatives and consequences will take two or three group sessions. In the first session the group helps the problem presenter write an initial list of alternative solutions. The group leader gives the problem presenter an assignment to interview at least three other people they know who have had similar problems and write down what they have done to solve the problem.

In the second group session the problem presenter brings back the list of alternative solutions. The group begins to ask questions about the logical consequences of using each alternative. Generally the group can easily identify alternative solutions that are based on irrational thinking and habitual self-defeating behavior that would make the problem worse. These failed alternatives need to be pointed out and eliminated from the list. The best three alternatives are identified. The problem presenter is given the assignment to project the best, worst, and most likely outcomes of those three alternative solutions.

In the third group session these logical outcomes are explored and the problem presenter moves into the next step of problem solving.

Step 3: Decision, Action, and Evaluation

The third and final step involves decision, action, and evaluation. With this information problem presenters must decide which alternative solution they will use. This can be accomplished by instructing the group to ask the following questions: "What alternatives do you plan to use to try to solve this problem? How will you put that solution into action (what steps are you going to take)? Who else needs to be involved in attempting to solve this problem? When will you take action? (Name a specific date and time.)"

They must then take action and try to solve the problem by using the identified alternative and evaluate if the alternative worked. Even when problems are carefully thought through, the alternative selected doesn't always work. If the alternative fails, it is eliminated from the list and a new alternative is chosen.

Evaluation usually takes place by asking the problem presenter the following questions: "What exactly did you do? How closely were you able to follow your original plan? How well did the attempted solution work? Was the problem solved or do you need to try another alternative?"

It may take more than one group to complete the decision, action, and evaluation step of problem solving. In the first group the person decides what alternatives he or she is going to use, then explains in detail how it will be implememented. Many times the group leader will use mental rehearsal or role-playing techniques to give the problem solver the opportunity to practice solving the problem in group before actually trying it in the real world.

The problem presenter may also be given an assignment to practice the solution in a safe environment before doing it for real. Such assignment could involve expressing anger to an AA sponsor before going home and attempting to express anger at a spouse. The person comes to the second group and reports on how the practice assignment went, discusses any concerns, and receives the assignment to try the solution for real. In the third group the problem presenter reports on how well the alternative worked.

Strategies for Solving Problems in Group

The problem-solving process requires multiple group sessions to solve a single target problem. This is why the group leader needs to have a coherent strategy for managing the resolution of a single target problem across a series of group sessions.

The problem identification and clarification phase usually requires two group sessions. In group #1 the problem presenter presents the problem and answers clarifying questions. He or she is assigned to write a clarified problem statement and present it in the next group. In group #2 the problem presenter presents the clarified problem statement to the group and is asked clarifying questions and given feedback. This usually results in a clear, concrete, and specific problem. The problem presenter is given the assignment to write a list of alternative solutions.

The identification of alternatives and consequences typically requires two groups. In group #3 the problem presenter presents alternative solutions and starts identifying consequences. He or she is assigned to interview three people who have solved similar problems and to bring their list of alternatives to the next group. In group #4 the problem presenter reviews the list of alternative solutions and explores the benefits and disadvantages of each. The best three alternatives are selected and the problem presenter is assigned to make a list of the best, worst, and most likely outcome in each of the three alternatives used.

The decision, action, and evaluation stage of problem solving usually takes three group sessions. In group #5 the problem presenter selects the best alternative and discusses or practices the steps required to implement the solution. He or she is given an assignment to practice the alternative solution in a safe and low-risk setting. In group #6 the problem presenter reports on difficulties and progress with the practice session. If things went well the assignment is given to use the alternative in a real-life situation. In group #7 the problem presenter reports on the outcome. If things went well and the problem is resolved, the process is finished. If the alternative did not work, the problem-solving attempt is reviewed and other alternative solutions are attempted until the problem is resolved.

The table on page 117 summarizes the group problem-solving process and how it unfolds over a series of groups.

This may seem like a tedious process, but it is absolutely essential if group members are to solve their problems permanently. As a general rule, people enter group therapy because they have poor problem-solving skills (they don't know how to solve problems), poor impulse control (they don't think things through before they act), poor self-discipline (they do what they want, when they want to, instead of following orderly processes that work), and difficulty in learning from past experience (they create a mess and never stop to think about what they did that caused it).

Group #	Group Action	Assignment
Step 1: Problem Identification and Clarification		
Group #1	Present problem and answer clarifying questions	Write a clarified problem statement
Group #2	Present clarified problem to group	Write a list of alternative solutions
Step 2: Identify Alternatives and Consequences		
Group #3	Present alternative solutions and start identifying consequences	Interview three people who have solved similar problems
Group #4	Review alternatives and select the best three	Project the best, worst, and most likely outcome to the three alternatives
Step 3: Decision, Action, Evaluation		
Group #5	Select best alternative and discuss or practice implementation	Practice alternative in safe and low-risk setting
Group #6	Report on problems and progress with practice sessions	Use the alternative in real-life situation
Group #7	Report on outcome	

As you can see, this problem-solving process addresses all of these issues by forcing group members to think things through before acting and to control the impulse to act out without thinking first. It also forces group members to evaluate what happened as a result of their actions and to begin identifying cause-and-effect relationships between what they do and what happens as a result. This means they are forced to start learning from their past experiences.

During a typical problem-solving session in a single group, two or three members will work on solving a problem. Each group member will work for twenty to forty minutes. The group leader usually gives the problem presenter about fifteen minutes to present the problem and respond to group questioning. The next fifteen minutes are reserved for feedback from group members and time for the group leader to summarize the feedback and work with the problem presenter to create an assignment to move to the next step in problem solving.

Focusing the Questioning Process on the Stage of Problem Solving

Step 1a: Problem Identification

- What is the problem and how is it affecting you?

Step 1b: Problem Clarification

- Who is involved in this problem?
- What are you or other people doing to cause or complicate the problem?
- When did this problem first start?
- Why are you interested in solving the problem right now? (Why didn't you solve it yesterday or put it off until tomorrow?)
- How is this problem affecting you or other people?
- Describe a past occurrence of this problem as if it were a story with a beginning, a middle, and an ending.
- Describe how this problem is likely to occur in the future.
- What other problems are there in your life that are similar to or related to this problem?
- How does this problem relate to your target disorder?
- Does this problem create an urge to relapse?
- Does this problem discourage you from practicing their recovery program?

Step 2a: Identifying Alternatives

- What methods have you used in the past to try and solve this problem?
- What was helpful? What was not helpful?
- What have other people with similar problems done to solve them?

118

- What new ideas can you think of to try and solve the problem?
- Write a list of the alternative solutions identified during the group.

Step 2b: Identifying the Consequences of Each Alternative

- What are the benefits and disadvantages of each alternative?
- Identify the three best alternative solutions.
- Analyze each of the top three alternatives by asking, "if I used each alternative ..."
  - What is the best that could happen?
  - What is the worst that could?
  - What is the most likely thing that probably will happen?

Step 3a: Decision

- What alternatives do you plan to use to try to solve this problem?.
- What steps will you take to put that solution into action?
- Who else needs to be involved in attempting to solve this problem?
- When will you take action? (Name a specific date and time.)
- What kind of preparation and support do you need to put the solution to work?

Step 3b: Action

- Did you do it?

Step 3c: Evaluation

- What exactly did you do?
- How closely were you able to follow your original plan?
- How well did the attempted solution work?
- Was the problem solved or do you need to try another alternative?

119

CHAPTER 9

Starting the First Problem-Solving Group

How the therapist conducts the first problem-solving group is often critical to the long-term success or failure of the group. This is especially true for a therapist who has an active group and wishes to change from other group therapy formats into a problem-solving format.

Many group therapists I have trained decided to implement the new group format gradually. This has failed almost universally. The group members become confused and actually have the worst of two worlds. They are still trying to maintain some of the old format group methods while trying to adapt to the new problem-solving group methods. I strongly recommend making the conversion all at once. Here is how the group therapists who have successfully converted their groups generally do it.

Step 1: Make a Decision and Get Training

The first thing to do is to carefully evaluate the problem-solving group format to see if it will meet your needs as a therapist and the needs of your group members. If you are convinced that it will, get some training. As mentioned earlier, an annual problem-solving group therapy workshop is conducted annually near Chicago, Illinois.

On-site training and consultation as well as low-cost audio and video tapes of that training are available.* Once you have read this book and either had training or have been exposed to actual examples of the group techniques, you are ready for step two.

Step 2: Announce the Change

Announce to your group that:

a. you have decided to change group formats because you believe the new format will be more helpful;

b. this session will be devoted to explaining the new format and teaching group members the basic problem-solving group skills; and

c. you hope all members will stay in group, but you will understand if they decide that the new format is not for them and you will assist them in transferring to a group that will meet their needs.

Remember that most group members are resistant to change and many will actively resist it. If you do not clearly and firmly announce the intent to change, the level of resistance to the new format will be very high.

Most group therapists make these announcements in a matter-of-fact "taking care of business" style. They inform the group and don't ask for permission. They also shift right into the training component without allowing much time for discussion. Here's what I recommend you say:

"Tonight I have an important announcement to make. After careful consideration I have decided to change the format of this therapy group into a problem-solving group format. This format is much more effective than the one we have been using. It will help each of you to quickly focus on and resolve the problems that have brought you to group. I've studied this group process and received training in it, and I know it will work well."

---

* For further information about these group therapy training packages or inservice training and consultation, contact The CENAPS Corporation, 18650 Dixie Highway, Homewood, IL 60430 (phone: 708/799-5000).

Step 3: Education about the Problem-Solving Group Process

"In this group I am going to explain how the new format works and give you an opportunity to try out some of the group skills. We will start with the new format in the next group session."

At this point the group therapist distributes and explains a series of handouts for orienting new members to group. These handouts explain:

1. The Primary Goal of Problem-Solving Group Therapy

The primary goal of problem-solving group therapy is to identify and resolve the target problems that caused members to enter the group and to change the irrational thoughts, unmanageable feelings, and self-defeating behaviors that drive those target problems.

2. The Group Responsibilities and Rules

Explain the group responsibilities and rules. This is done by giving each group member a copy of the rules, reading them out loud using a round-robin technique, and inviting questions, comments, or examples.

3. The Standard Problem-Solving Group Format

Explain the standard group format. This is best done by giving copies of the short description of the process, explaining each of the eight parts of the format, and allowing questions and comments.

4. The Seven Core Group Member Skills

Explain the seven core skills that group members need to learn. This is best done by taking each skill, explaining it, demonstrating it, and when possible letting group members practice it. The seven core skills are:

4–1. Centering and immediate stress management. Group members need to learn how to monitor and manage their stress in the group. This is done by helping group members imagine a stress thermometer that starts in the pit of their stomach and ends in their throat. The lowest reading (0) reflects deep, gut-level relaxation that is so complete you want to fall asleep. The highest rating (10) indicates such intense stress that you feel like you are about to have a convulsion. At a stress level 7 or 8, the stress becomes so intense that people have to defend themselves against it by either getting defensive, shutting down, or defocusing from the issue that is creating the stress.

There are two goals of immediate stress management training. The first goal is to teach self-monitoring techniques that allow group members to recognize when they are about to shut down because their personal stress level is approaching 7 or 8. The second goal is to teach rapid relaxation response techniques that can quickly lower the stress level so the individual can continue to think and talk about the problem without getting defensive, shutting down, or changing the subject.

Spend five minutes taking the group through a typical immediate relaxation response training session. You can use any one of a variety of techniques. The one I find most effective is called the **Magic Triangle Relaxation Method.** A script for guiding patients through this centering technique is on page 85. This training will help group members to get centered during the opening procedure.

4–2. Giving a reaction. Group members learn how to give a reaction by reporting what they thought about last group, how they felt about last group, and the three people who stood out and why. Explain this simple procedure, give an example, and have each group member practice giving a reaction.

4–3. Developing, completing, and reporting on homework assignments. Explain to the group that the goal is for group members to do things differently between group sessions. To accomplish that goal all group members will be expected to develop and actively work at completing homework assignments. Typical assignments will involve reading, journaling, writing lists, and interviewing other people or group members. Ask group members to identify some of the things they have done in the past that could be used as assignments when using the new format.

4–4. Presenting problems. The key to solving problems in group is to identify and present problem issues and work at resolving them using the standard problem-solving process. Explain the four steps of presenting a problem in group (problem presentation, group questioning, group feedback, summary and assignment). Then explain the three steps of the standard problem-solving process (problem identification and clarification; identifying alternatives and consequences; and decision, action, and evaluation). Ask group members to think about the problems they are currently working on and see if they can figure out what stage of the problem-solving process they are currently in.

4-5. Asking and responding to clarifying questions. Group questioning is a critical skill for group members because it forces problem presenters to think about their problems in different and more helpful ways. Group members need to learn two mirror-image skills related to group questioning. The first skill is how to ask clear, relevant, and intelligent questions. They use this skill when helping other group members solve problems. The second skill is learning how to respond to clarifying questions without becoming guarded or defensive. They will use this skill when presenting problems and inviting other group members to ask clarifying questions.

4-6. Giving and receiving feedback. There are also two group skills related to feedback. The first is how to give clear, concise feedback using the standard format. The standard format completes these two statements: "After listening to you, I think your problem is ..."; and "After listening to you, the way I feel about you is ...". The goal is to say what you mean in a short and easy-to-understand way. The second skill involves learning how to listen to feedback without becoming defensive. Group members learn how to use active listening to make sure they hear and understand the feedback and learn to just listen without having to defend or respond to what is said.

4-7. Completing the closure exercise. At the end of the session, each group member answers three questions: What is the most important thing I learned in this group? What am I going to do differently as a result of what I learned? What assignment am I working on?

Step 4: Give a Problem Identification and Clarification Assignment

Ask each group member to identify the target problem they want to solve in group. Explain that the target problem is the core or most important issue that made them enter the group. Describe the format for presenting the problem by completing four statements: "The target problem I want to work on in group is ..."; "This first became a problem for me when ..."; "I have tried to solve the problem in the past by ..."; and "The self-defeating behavior I have used in the past to try and cope with this problem is ...".

Each group member is asked to think about and write out the completion of these statements. They are told that the next problem-solving group will begin with a round-robin exercise in which each group member will present their target problem. You will then set the agenda by asking, "Who wants to start working on their target problem?"

Step 5: Conduct the First Problem-Solving Group Session

Start the next group session by asking each group member to present his or her target problem to the group. Keep each presentation to about two or three minutes. The goal is not to solve these problems; it is for the group members to begin self-disclosing and getting people to start volunteering to work on problems in group.

After everyone has reviewed his or her problem, ask, "Who wants to work in group?" Set the agenda and begin the problem-solving process. Close the group with the closure exercise. Announce that the next group will begin with reactions to the last session.

Starting New Members in Group

Problem-solving groups are most effective when they are **open-ended.** This means that group members are continually entering and leaving the group. By having open-ended groups, new members who apply for the group can enter immediately while their motivation to identify and resolve problems is high. Most importantly, there are many group members at different stages of maturity in the problem-solving process. As a result new members can see older members model group skills and problem-solving procedures. Older members can reinforce their skills and build self-esteem by helping new members learn the ropes.

When a new member enters the group, he or she needs to have identified a target problem to work on in group. This is typically done during the screening process or in an individual session before the new member enters group. They are asked to introduce them-selves (twenty-five words or less) and briefly explain their target problem. The whole introduction should take less than three minutes.

The therapist then has the group review the rules, responsibili-ties, and corrective procedures. This reinforces them for all group members. New group members are told they can observe or partici-pate in any way they are comfortable. They will be expected to complete the closure exercise and bring a reaction with them to the next group session. They are not expected to present a problem in the first group session. This gives the new member an opportunity to observe and see how the group functions. Most new members roll up their sleeves and get started right away.

Evaluating Group Therapy Leadership Skills

As can be seen, conducting problem-solving group therapy is a skill-based activity. Conducting problem-solving groups requires the development of fourteen specific skills. These specific skill areas can be used for the purpose of self-evaluation or they can be used as supervisory and evaluation criteria for clinical staff who are running groups. The following questionnaire* will help you evaluate how skilled you are at using the standard problem-solving group format.

---

* This questionnaire was developed in 1992 by Terence T. Gorski and The CENAPS Corporation for use at its annual Problem-Solving Group Therapy Course conducted in Chicago, Illinois. It is copyrighted by Terence T. Gorski and may not be reproduced without written permission. For further information, contact The CENAPS Corporation, 18650 Dixie Highway, Homewood, IL 60430 (phone: 708/799-5000).

1. *Treatment Planning:* How are your skills at developing an individual treatment plan that identifies a target problem, a goal, and a sequence of group interventions for achieving that goal based on the stages of the standard problem-solving process?

Excellent   Good   Fair   Poor

2. *Preparation before Group:* How are your skills at preparing for group by reviewing the individual treatment plan, the target problems, and specific sequence of interventions designed to solve the problem?

Excellent   Good   Fair   Poor

3. *Opening Procedure:* How are your skills at using an opening procedure to set an effective group climate within the first fifteen minutes of the group session?

Excellent   Good   Fair   Poor

4. *Eliciting Reactions:* How are your skills at eliciting clear reactions from group members about the previous group?

Excellent   Good   Fair   Poor

5. *Reporting on Assignments:* How are your skills at guiding group members in briefly reporting on progress and problems in completing therapeutic assignments?

Excellent   Good   Fair   Poor

6. *Setting the Agenda:* How are your skills at setting the group agenda by determining which group members will work in each group?

Excellent   Good   Fair   Poor

7. *Problem Presentation:* How are your skills at motivating group members to present and clarify problems clearly and concisely to the group?

Excellent   Good   Fair   Poor

8. *Group Questioning:* How are your skills at motivating and guiding group members to ask appropriate clarifying questions?

Excellent   Good   Fair   Poor

9. *Group Feedback:* How are your skills at motivating and guiding group members to give clear, honest feedback, both positive and negative in a supportive and proactive manner?

Excellent   Good   Fair   Poor

10. *Giving Assignments:* How are your skills at giving and monitoring the completion of appropriate therapy assignments that keep the client focused on resolving the target problem..

Excellent   Good   Fair   Poor

11. *Group Closure:* How are your skills at providing appropriate closure at the end of each group session that focuses group members on the primary thing they learned in the group session and what they are going to do differently as a result of what they learned?

Excellent   Good   Fair   Poor

12. *Group Review and Evaluation:* How are your skills at reviewing and evaluating group progress and problems at the end of each group?

Excellent   Good   Fair   Poor

13. *Pacing:* How are your skills at maintaining a productive pace in group that is fast enough to avoid boredom but slow enough to avoid frustration?

Excellent   Good   Fair   Poor

14. *Documenting:* How are your skills at documenting what happens in group in an accurate and time-efficient manner that allows objective measurement of progress toward problem resolution?

Excellent   Good   Fair   Poor

15. *Strengths:* After reviewing my answers to the above questions, my three primary strengths as a problem-solving group leader are:

(1) _____

(2) _____

(3) _____

16. *Weaknesses:* After reviewing my answers to the above questions, my three primary weaknesses as a problem-solving group leader are:

(1) _____

(2) _____

(3) _____

17. *Action Plan:* The steps that I am going to take to improve my skills as a problem-solving group leader are:

_____

_____

_____

_____

_____

A Final Word

Problem-solving group therapy is an exciting and challenging way to conduct groups. The method is highly structured yet flexible enough to allow both group leaders and group members to approach their problems creatively.

This book was designed to give you practical guidelines for starting and running these types of groups. I hope you feel prepared to improve and perfect your brief strategic problem-solving group therapy skills.

The Group Therapy Tool Kit

The following section provides group therapists with a number of tools that will help them to implement problem-solving group therapy. This Group Therapy Tool Kit* is available in a separate publication that makes access to these simple and easy to use. It includes the following:

- Group Responsibilities

- Group Rules

- Group Corrective Procedures

- Problem-Solving Group Agenda: A Description

- Problem-Solving Group Agenda: An Outline for Group Leaders

- Problem-Solving Group Agenda: An Outline for Group Members

---

*Developed by Terence T. Gorski
© Copyright, 1995, Terence T. Gorski, CENAPS, 18650 Dixie Highway, Homewood, IL 60430
(phone: 708/799-5000)

Group Responsibilities

As a group member you are responsible for:

1. *Giving a reaction to last session by telling the group:* (a) what you thought about last group; (b) how you felt about last group; and (c) the three group members who stood out to you and why they stood out.
2. *Completing and reporting on assignments* to help you make progress in problem solving.
3. *Presenting problems to the group* at least once every third group session.
4. *Listening* while other group members are discussing their problems, reporting what you heard them say, and asking them if you understood correctly.
5. *Asking clarifying questions* when other group members are presenting problems.
6. *Giving feedback* to other members who are working on problems by telling the group member what you think his or her problem is and how you feel about him or her as a person.
7. *Completing the closure exercise* at the end of each group by reporting the most important thing that was learned during that group and what you intend to do differently as a result of what you learned.

Group Rules

The basic rules for problem-solving group therapy are:

1. *Attendance and Punctuality:* Group members are responsible for attending all group sessions, arriving on time, and staying for the full group session.
2. *Compliance with Basic Responsibilities:* Membership in the group implies a willingness to comply with the seven basic group responsibilities described above.
3. *Freedom of Participation:* Within the constraints of the standard format and basic responsibilities, you can say anything you want, anytime you want to say it. Other group members have the right to give you feedback about what you say and how you say it. Silence is not a virtue in this group and can be antitherapeutic.
4. *Right of Refusal:* With the exception of refusing to comply with basic group responsibilities, you can refuse to answer any question or complete any assignment. The group members cannot force you to participate, but they do have the right to express how they feel about your silence or your choice not to get involved.
5. *Confidentiality:* What happens in the group stays among the members, with the exception of the group leaders who may consult with other members of the treatment team in order to provide more effective treatment and who may report any inappropriate behavior or violation of rules and responsibilities to the appropriate authority. Group members agree not to discuss the content of the problems presented by the other group members with anyone else.
6. *No Violence:* Acting out with physical or verbal violence within the group may be grounds for dismissal. Physical violence includes pushing, shoving, or hitting other group members. Verbal violence involves making threats, yelling, using profane language, and name calling. The threat of violence is as good as the act.

7. *No Dating, Romantic Involvement, or Sexual Involvement:* Dating, romantic involvement, or sexual involvement among group members is not allowed. Such activities can sabotage one or both persons' treatment. If such involvement starts to develop, it is to be brought to the attention of the group or your individual counselor at once.

8. *Communication before Termination:* Anyone who decides to leave the group has a responsibility to inform the group in person before leaving.

Group Corrective Procedures

If you fail to meet your group responsibilities or violate group rules, the following corrective discipline procedures will be used:

Step 1: The Verbal Warning: You will be told directly that you are not meeting your responsibilities or that you are violating group rules, then asked if you recognize the problem and are willing to correct it.

Step 2. Group Problem-Solving and Feedback: If you continue to have a problem with the rules and responsibilities, you will be asked to work on this problem in group.

Step 3: Suspension or Termination from Group: If you still cannot or will not comply with the basic rules and responsibilities, you will not be allowed to continue in group.

Problem-Solving Group Agenda: A Description

The standard eight-item agenda for problem-solving group therapy consists of:

1. Preparation
2. Opening Procedure
3. Reactions to Last Session
4. Report on Assignments
5. Setting the Agenda
6. Problem-Solving Group Process
7. Closure Exercise
8. Review and Evaluation

1. *Preparation:* Group members are expected to prepare for group by identifying problems and completing therapy assignments.
2. *Opening Procedure:* The group leader enters the group room and asks the group members to arrange the chairs so everyone can easily see one another. New group members are briefly introduced. The group leader takes attendance and has a short interaction with each group member. The group leader conducts a centering technique that helps group members relax, notice their current thoughts and feelings, remember what happened in the last session, and remember which group members stood out to them and why.
3. *Reactions to Last Session:* The group leader asks the group members to give a two-minute reaction to the last session by completing these statements:
   • What I thought about the last group session is...;
   • How I felt about the last group session is...; and
   • The three group members (other than the therapists) who stood out to me from last session were...and why they stood out is....
   When giving a reaction, the group members are asked to talk directly to the person they are reacting to, using the first person. An example would be: "John, you stood out to me because you were able to challenge the group leader. I would have been too afraid to do that and I respect you for it."

136

4. **Report on Assignments:** Each group member is asked to give a one-minute report on their assignment by answering the following questions:
   - What was your assignment?
   - Did you complete the assignment? If yes, do you want time to work on the results in group? If no, why not and when will it be completed?
5. **Setting the Agenda:** The therapist sets the agenda by asking, "Who has an issue or assignment to work on in group?" The group leader will ask for a brief, thirty-second description of the problem and will ask if this is an emergency issue that must be dealt with immediately. The therapist identifies all members who want to work and sets the order in which people will work. Group members who do not have time to complete their work in this group session will be first on the agenda in the following group session.
6. **Problem-Solving Process:** One person works at a time with the entire group involved in the problem-solving process. A standard problem-solving process is used that consists of several steps: These are:
   - *Problem Presentation:* The problem presenter (the group member who is processing a problem in group) describes his or her problem to the group. The initial presentation of the problem is often vague, general, and incomplete. The member is asked several times, "Is there anything else we need to know to help you solve the problem?" When the member either begins repeating or states he or she doesn't have anything else, the group begins to ask clarifying questions.
   - *Questioning by the Group:* The group asks clarifying questions using an active listening model. Each group member asks a question, listens to the answer, tells the problem presenter what they heard, and confirms if they heard it correctly. The goal of group questioning is to identify the irrational thoughts, unmanageable feelings, and self-defeating action urges and behaviors that are related to the

problem that the problem presenter may not be aware of.

- *Feedback from Group Members:* Each group member gives feedback to the member who worked by answering two questions: (1) What do you think is the core problem of the person who worked? (2) How do you feel about the person who worked?
- *Processing and Assignment by the Therapist:* The therapist summarizes the feedback and helps the problem presenter develop an assignment that will help him or her progress in the problem-solving process.

  During problem-solving each group member has the responsibility to: (1) listen to other group members' problems; (2) ask questions to clarify the problem or proposed solution; and (3) give feedback about what they think the problem is and how they feel about the group member presenting the problem.

7. *Closure Exercise:* About fifteen minutes before the end of the group session, the leader stops the problem-solving process and passes out the Closure Exercise Worksheet, which asks three questions: (1) What is the most important thing you learned in this group? (2) What are you going to do differently as a result of what you learned? and (3) What is the group assignment you will be working on for future group presentation? Each group member briefly (one minute or less) reports his or her answer to each question. The group leader writes a group note on the bottom of each worksheet for entry in the record. The time and place of the next group are confirmed and group is adjourned.

8. *Review and Evaluation:* Group members are encouraged to meet informally after the group to discuss their feelings and reactions to the group therapy session.

Problem-Solving Group Agenda: An Outline for Group Leaders

The standard eight-item agenda for problem-solving group therapy consists of:

1. Preparation	5. Setting the Agenda
2. Opening Procedure	6. Problem-Solving Group Process
3. Reactions to Last Session	7. Closure Exercise
4. Report on Assignments	8. Review and Evaluation

1. **Preparation**
   - Review basic information, treatment plan, and current assigment of each group member.
2. **Opening Procedure**
   - Circle the chairs so that group members can see each other easily.
   - Briefly introduce new group members.
   - Check in with each group member and take attendance.
   - Complete the centering technique (relaxation exercise, mental review of last session and what happened since, mental preparation for reactions).
3. **Reactions to Last Session**
   - What I thought about the last group session is ....
   - How I felt about the last group session is ....
   - The three group members (other than the therapists) who stood out to me from last session and why they stood out are....
4. **Report on Assignments**
   - What was your assignment?
   - Did you complete the assignment? (If yes, do you want time to work on the results in group? If no, why not and when will it be completed?)
5. **Setting the Agenda**
   - Ask: Who wants to work?
   - Ask: What do you want to work on?

- Ask: Is this an emergency?
- Decide: Order in which group members will work.

6. **Problem-Solving Process**
   - Problem Presentation: Tell the group what you want to work on.
   - Questioning by the Group:
     A. Active listening model of clarification
        (1) Ask a question.
        (2) Listen to the answer.
        (3) Tell what you heard ("What I heard you say is ...").
        (4) Confirm if you heard it correctly ("Did I hear you correctly?").
     B. Guide the problem presenter through the problem-solving process:
        (1) Identify and clarify the problem.
           - Who, what, when, where, why, and how?
           - Related thoughts, feelings, behaviors, and relationships
           - Relationship to target disorder (CD, personality or mental disorder)
        (2) Identify alternatives and logical consequences.
           - Accept personal responsibility and stop blaming others.
           - Review past efforts to solve the problem.
           - Brainstorm new ideas, options, and alternatives.
           - Determine benefits and disadvantages of each alternative.
           - Project the best, worst, and most likely outcomes of each.
        (3) Decision, action, evaluation
           - Mental rehearsal
           - Practice in a safe environment (role play and home work)
           - Taking action in the real world
   - Feedback from Group Members:

A. After listening to you, I think your problem is....

B. After listening to you, the way I feel about you is....

- Summary and Assignment by the Therapist

A. Summarize the feedback.

B. Develop an assignment.

7. **Closure Exercise**
   - What is the most important thing you learned in this group?
   - What are you going to do differently as a result of what you learned?
   - What assignment are you working on?

8. **Review and Evaluation**
   - Progress and problems
   - Personal reactions to the group session

Problem-Solving Group Agenda:
An Outline for Group Members

1. **Preparation**
   - Complete assignments and prepare a reaction to last session.
2. **Opening Procedure**
   - Circle the chairs so group members can see each other easily.
   - Briefly introduce new group members.
   - Check in with each group member and take attendance.
   - Complete the centering technique (relaxation exercise, mental review of last session and what happened since, mental preparation for reactions).
3. **Reactions to Last Session**
   - What I thought about the last group session is ....
   - How I felt about the last group session is ....
   - The three group members (other than the therapists) who stood out to me from last session and why they stood out are....
4. **Report on Assignments**
   - What was your assignment?
   - Did you complete the assignment? (If yes, do you want time to work on the results in group? If no, why not and when will it be completed?)
5. **Setting the Agenda**
   - Volunteer to work.
   - Briefly explain what you want to work on.
6. **Problem-Solving Process**
   - Problem Presentation: Tell the group what you want to work on.
   - Questioning by the Group:
     (1) Ask a question.
     (2) Listen to the answer.
     (3) Tell what you heard ("What I heard you say is ...").
     (4) Confirm if you heard it correctly ("Did I hear you correctly?").

- Feedback from Group Members:
  (1) After listening to you, I think your problem is....
  (2) After listening to you, the way I feel about you is ....
- Summary and Assignment by the Therapist
  (1) Summarize the feedback.
  (2) Develop an assignment.

7. **The Closure Exercise**
   - What is the most important thing you learned in this group?
   - What are you going to do differently as a result of what you learned?
   - What assignment are you working on?

8. **Review and Evaluation**
   - Progress and problems
   - Personal reactions to the group session

References

1. Eric Berne, *Principles of Group Treatment* (New York: Grove Press, 1966).
2. S. B. Blume, "Group Psychotherapy in the Treatment of Alcoholism." In S. Zimberg, J. Wallace, and S. B. Blume, eds., *Practical Approaches to Alcoholism Psychotherapy* (New York: Plenum Press, 1978).
3. Charles H. Browning and Beverly J. Browning, *How to Partner with Managed Care* (Independence, Missouri: Herald House/Independence Press, 1995).
4. E. M. Brunner-Orne and M. Orne, "Directive Group Therapy in the Treatment of Alcoholism: Technique and Rationale," *International Journal of Group Psychotherapy* 4 (1954): 272-279.
5. Simon H. Busman and Alan S. Gurman, *The Theory and Practice of Brief Therapy* (New York: Guilford Press, 1988).
6. Brian Cade and William Hudson O'Hanlon, *A Brief Guide to Brief Therapy* (New York: Norton and Company, 1993).
7. D. R. Dorof, "Group Psychotherapy in Alcoholism Treatment and Rehabilitation of Chronic Alcoholism." In B. Kissin and H. Begetter, eds., *Biology of Alcoholism*, vol. 5 (New York: Plenum Press, 1977).
8. G. S. Evseeff, "Group Psychotherapy in the State Hospital," *Dis. Nervous System* 9 (1948): 214-218.
9. R. Fox, "Group Psychotherapy with Alcoholics," *International Journal of Group Psychotherapy* 12 (1962): 56-63.
10. Terence T. Gorski, *Workshop Manual: Alcoholism and Group Treatment: A Comprehensive Overview* (Homewood, Illinois: CENAPS Corporation, 1979).
11. Terence T. Gorski, *Keeping the Balance: A Psychospiritual Model of Recovery* (Independence, Missouri: Herald House/Independence Press, 1992).
12. Terence T. Gorski and Merlene M. Miller, *Staying Sober: A Guide for Relapse Prevention* (Independence, Missouri: Herald House/Independence Press, 1986).

13. Terence T. Gorski, *The Staying Sober Workbook* (Independence, Missouri: 1992).
14. Terence T. Gorski, *Passages Through Recovery: An Action Plan for Preventing Relapse* (Center City, Minnesota: Hazelden, 1989).
15. H. Greenbaum, "Group Psychotherapy with Alcoholics in Conjunction with Antabuse Treatment," *International Journal of Group Psychotherapy* 4 (1954): 30–45.
16. A. Haber, A. Paley, and A. Block, "Treatment of Problem Drinking at Winters Veterans Administration Hospital," *Bulletin of the Menninger Clinic* 13 (1949): 24–30.
17. R. Heath, "Psychotherapy of Alcohol Addiction," *Quarterly Journal on Studies on Alcoholism* 5 (1945): 555–562.
18. O. Martensen-Larsen, "Group Psychotherapy with Alcoholics in Private Practice," *International Journal of Group Psychotherapy* 6 (1956): 28–37.
19. H. Mullan and I. Sanguiliano, *Alcoholism, Group Psychotherapy and Rehabilitation* (Springfield, Illinois: Charles C. Thomas, 1966).
20. William Hudson O'Hanlon and Michele Weiner-Davis, *In Search of Solutions: A New Direction in Psychotherapy* (New York: W. W. Norton and Co., 1989).
21. Irvin D. Yalom, *The Theory and Practice of Group Psychotherapy* (New York: Basic Books, 1970).
22. Sheldon Zimberg, M.D., *The Clinical Management of Alcoholism* (New York: Brunner/Mazel Publishers, 1982), 81–85.

THREE-DAY TRAINING
in PROBLEM SOLVING
GROUP THERAPY

The CENAPS Model of Problem Solving Group Therapy is based on the most advanced clinical procedures to help clinicians improve their group therapy skills. Spend three days in this workshop with Terence Gorski as he guides you through a unique skills training process.

Problem Solving Group Therapy is brief, targeted, and strategic. It meets the needs of managed care providers who are seeking brief interventions.

- Empowers therapists to work effectively in the managed care environment.
- Simplifies charting by building documentation into the group process.
- Meets the needs of managed care providers with a standardized model of group therapy.

Who should attend?
- Addiction Counselors
- EAP Counselors
- Private Practitioners
- Psychologists

- Program Managers
- Probation Counselors
- Case Managers
- Social Workers

Continuing Education Units available.

For more information contact:

The CENAPS Corporation
18650 Dixie Highway
Homewood, Illinois 60430
(708) 799-5000
Fax (708) 799-5032

STAYING SOBER RECOVERY EDUCATION MODULES
by Terence T. Gorski and Merlene Miller   ISBN 0-8309-0542-1

This is a ready-to-use and easily adaptable professional education program for recovery and relapse prevention. It is a vital tool that provides a quick and easy way to design and execute in-service staff training and patient education sessions.

What do you get in the modules?
- A guide to adult learning principles
- Session goals and objectives
- Detailed lecture outlines complete with examples
- Pre- and post-tests
- Educational exercises
- Copy for 300 professionally designed overhead transparencies

Easily adapted to an eight-session basic overview course or a 32-session comprehensive review.   17-016650 (Modules)
17-018860 (Exercise Manual)

To order: Call 1-800-767-8181
In Canada call 1-800-373-8382

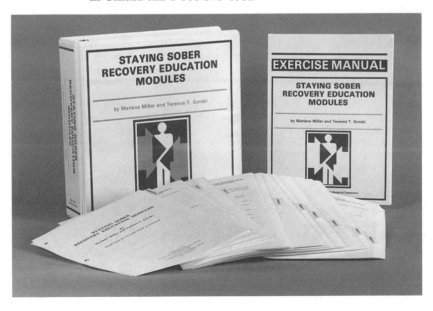

PROBLEM SOLVING GROUP THERAPY

Audio- and Videotapes by Terence T. Gorski

Tape 1: BASIC PRINCIPLES OF GROUP THERAPY
- Definition of group therapy
- Cognitive, affective, and behavioral goals
- Four types of therapy groups process
- Six characteristics of effective group therapy
- Balancing process and content
- Role of therapist and cotherapist
- Optimum group size and duration of sessions

17-026064	Audio
17-026074	Video

Tape 2: INTEGRATING GROUP THERAPY WITH OTHER MODALITIES
- How the group relates to individual therapy, self-help groups, recovery education, and family therapy
- Psychological support and confrontation
- The 80/20 rule of group participation
- Note taking and tape recording
- Managing dysfunctional members

17-026065	Audio
17-026075	Video

Tape 3: SPECIALTY GROUPS FOR CHEMICAL DEPENDENCY PATIENTS
- Special problems of chemical dependency patients
- Sobriety and other addiction-specific goals
- Basic requirements for chemical dependency recovery
- The recovery process and group goals
- Specialty groups based on stage of recovery
- Admission and discharge criteria for groups

17-026066	Audio
17-026076	Video

Tape 4: THE PROBLEM SOLVING GROUP THERAPY PROTOCOL
- Group member's responsibilities
- Group rates
- Standard group agenda

17-026067	Audio
17-026077	Video

Tape 5: PROBLEM SOLVING GROUP THERAPY DEMONSTRATION
- Live demonstration, discussion, and questions

17-026068	Audio
17-026078	Video

Tape 6: PREPARATION AND WARM-UP PROCEDURE
- Lecture, demonstration, practice, and feedback

17-026069	Audio
17-026079	Video

Tape 7: PROBLEM SOLVING GROUP PROCEDURE, PART 1
- Lecture, demonstration, practice, and feedback

17-026070	Audio
17-026080	Video

Tape 8: PROBLEM SOLVING GROUP PROCEDURE, PART 2
- Lecture, demonstration, practice, and feedback

17-026071	Audio
17-026081	Video

Tape 9: CLOSURE AND DEBRIEFING
- Lecture, demonstration, practice, and feedback

17-026072	Audio
17-026082	Video

SET OF NINE TAPES:

17-026073	Audio
17-026083	Video

To order: Call 1-800-767-8181
In Canada call 1-800-373-8382